THE PLAYFAIR HOURS

Omine labia mea a
perics. Et os meum
annüciabit laude tuā.

THE PLAYFAIR HOURS

A Late Fifteenth Century Illuminated Manuscript from Rouen (V&A, L.475–1918)

ROWAN WATSON

VICTORIA AND ALBERT MUSEUM

Published by the Victoria and Albert Museum, 1984,
with The Folio Society and Readers Union
Designed by Patrick Yapp
Printed in Great Britain by Westerham Press

ISBN 0 905209 98 2

Frontispiece: FIGURE I The Crucifixion.
Edinburgh University Library, MS.306, folio 47 recto.

In Memoriam

Joseph Harold Armfield (1889–1981)
Gertrude Mary Armfield, *née* Uttley (1884–1983)

Acknowledgements

I would like to thank the following for help and advice: Janet Backhouse, Jayne Cook, Mirjam Foot, Michael Gullick, Dr J.T.D. Hall, Michael Holmes, John Hopkins, Dr A. Korteweg, R.W. Lightbown, John Plummer, N. Rogers and P. Woudhuysen. I am particularly indebted to John Higgitt for directing me to two manuscripts linked with the Playfair Hours (The Yester Hours in Magdalene College, Cambridge, and the Farmor Hours in The Hague).

Figures 6, 9, 12, 13, 16, 21, 27, 28 and 29 are reproduced by permission of the Curators of the Bodleian Library, Oxford; figures 5, 7 and 11 by permission of the Syndics of the Cambridge University Library; figures 1, 3, 4, 14, 15, 18, 19, 23, and 24 by permission of the Edinburgh University Library; figure 30 by permission of the Syndics of the Fitzwilliam Museum, Cambridge; figures 8, 20, 22 and 26 by permission of the National Library of Scotland; figures 2 and 17 by permission of the Society of Antiquaries, London.

Contents

Abbreviations for Principal Manuscripts Referred to, with Notes

Antiquaries 13   Society of Antiquaries, London, MS.13. Book of Hours, Use of
                    Rouen. See N.R. Ker, *Medieval Manuscripts in British Libraries*, vol.I
                    (Oxford, 1969), p.296.

Buchanan e 3   Bodleian Library, Oxford, MS. Buchanan e 3. Book of Hours, Use
                    of Rouen. See O. Pächt & J.J.G. Alexander, *Illuminated Manuscripts
                    in the Bodleian Library, Oxford*, vol.I (Oxford, 1966), p.63 (no.807)
                    and plate LIX (folio 74, Virgin and Child, with owner portrait).

Buchanan e 13   Bodleian Library, Oxford, MS. Buchanan e 13. Book of Hours, Use
                    of Rouen. See Pächt & Alexander, *Illuminated Manuscripts*, vol.I,
                    p.59 (no.752).

CUL Add.4099   Cambridge University Library, Additional MS.4099. Book of Hours,
                    Use of Rouen.

Douce 72   Bodleian Library, Oxford, MS. Douce 72. Book of Hours, Use of
                    Rouen. See *Summary Catalogue of Western Manuscripts in the Bodleian
                    Library*, no.21646; Pächt & Alexander, *Illuminated Manuscripts*, vol.I,
                    p.65 (no.843) and plate LXI (folio 76, Virgin and Child enthroned).

Douce 253   Bodleian Library, Oxford, MS. Douce 253. Book of Hours, Use of
                    Rouen. See *Summary Catalogue*, no.21827; Pächt & Alexander, *Illu-
                    minated Manuscripts*. vol.I, p.59, (no.753) and plate LVIII (folio 18,
                    Tree of Jesse).

EUL 43   Edinburgh University Library, MS.43. See C.R. Borland, *A Descrip-
                    tive Catalogue of the Western Medieval Manuscripts in Edinburgh Univer-
                    sity Library* (Edinburgh, 1916), pp.73–78, with plate (folio 6 verso,
                    calendar illustration for June); *Angels, Nobles and Unicorns. Art and
                    Patronage in Medieval Scotland* [catalogue of an exhibition held in the
                    National Museum of Scotland] (1982), pp.86–87 (no.E63), with
                    plate (folio 25 verso, Coronation of Virgin, with Virgin and Child
                    in gold mandorla).

EUL 306   Edinburgh University Library, MS.306. See N.R. Ker, *Medieval
                    Manuscripts in British Libraries*, vol.II (Oxford, 1977), pp.598–599;

Manuscript Treasures in Edinburgh University Library. An Album of Illustrations, compiled by J.T.D. Hall (Edinburgh, 1980), colour plate 10 (folio 53, David in penitence, with David slaying Goliath in lower register).

Farmor Hours — Koninklijke Bibliotheek, The Hague, MS.133 D16. Book of Hours, Use of Sarum. See *Catalogus Codicum Manuscriptorum Bibliothecae Regiae. Vol.I: Libri Theologici* (The Hague, 1922), p.49; *Liturgische handschriften uit de Koninklijke Bibliotheek* (The Hague: Rijksmuseum Meermanno-Westreenianum), 1983, p.36 (cat.no.68) and p.67 (plate of folio 38, Annunciation to the Shepherds).

Fitzwilliam 76 — Fitzwilliam Museum, MS.76. Book of Hours, Use of Rouen. See M.R. James, *A Descriptive Catalogue of the Manuscripts in the Fitzwilliam Museum* (Cambridge, 1895), pp.200–201.

Fitzwilliam 106 — Fitzwilliam Museum, Cambridge, MS.106. Book of Hours, Use of Rouen. See James, *Descriptive Catalogue*, pp.247–249.

NLS 6129 — National Library of Scotland, Edinburgh, MS.6129. Book of Hours, Use of Rouen. See Ker, *Medieval Manuscripts in British Libraries*, vol.II, p.528.

NLS 6131 — National Library of Scotland, Edinburgh, MS.6131. Book of Hours, Use of Rouen. See Ker, *loc.cit.*

Playfair Hours — Victoria and Albert Museum, London, L.475–1918. Book of Hours, Use of Sarum. See *Victoria and Albert Museum. Review of the Principal Acquisitions During the Year 1918* (London: HMSO, 1920), pp.30–31 and plates 11 & 12 (folio 169 verso, the Wound of Christ; folio 170, text); J. Harthan, *Books of Hours and their Owners* (1977), pp.25, 27 (plates of folios 1 verso–2 recto, 4 verso–5 recto, 8 verso–9 recto, and 12 verso–13 recto, calendar illustrations for February, May and September with zodiac sign of preceding month, zodiac sign of December with four Evangelists); *Angels, Nobles and Unicorns* (Edinburgh: National Museum of Scotland, 1982), pp.85–6 (no.E61), with plate (folio 36, Annunciation).

Yester Hours — Magdalene College, Cambridge, Pepys Library, MS.1576. Book of Hours, Use of Sarum. See M.R. James, *Bibliotheca Pepysiana. A Descriptive Catalogue of the Library of Samuel Pepys. Part III. Medieval Manuscripts* (1923), pp.14–19.

I. *Introduction*

BOOKS of Hours are the best known category of book associated with the medieval centuries in the west. By the fourteenth century they were replacing the Psalter as the book preferred for the private devotions of the individual, and in the fifteenth century they were mass produced in large quantities for what seems to have been an ever-expanding market. Some idea of the demand can be gained from early printed Books of Hours, which unlike the manuscript variety are liable to contain information about the date, place and people by whom they were made: 760 editions of such works are known to have been published between 1485 and 1530, the great majority of them in Paris. The number of surviving manuscript Books of Hours that are illuminated in some way and datable to the late fifteenth and early sixteenth century shows that traditional methods of book production also played a part in meeting this demand during these years, perhaps devoting itself to what today would be called a particular sector of the market.[1]

Aristocratic and wealthy patrons could employ the most famous artists of the day to illustrate Books of Hours, so that books of this kind bulk large in discussions of stylistic change in the history of medieval art. The work of Jean Pucelle (d.1333/4) is best known from the books he illustrated for members of the royal court in France. The Duc de Berry had the Limburg brothers on his payroll until 1416. The Books of Hours produced for this prince are perhaps as well known today as to fifteenth century bibliophile courtiers. Much of the work of painters such as Fouquet (d.1475/1482) or Bourdichon (d.1520/1521), both of whom had status at the royal court as painters to the king of France, comes down to us in illuminated manuscripts.

The Playfair Hours (the name derives from twentieth century Scottish owners of the manuscript) represents a very different class of book from those just mentioned. We know very little about who was responsible for making the

⚜ FIGURE 2 The Annunciation to the Shepherds.
Society of Antiquaries, London, MS.13, folio 51 recto.

book and, indeed, for whom it was made. Rather it is one of a large number of books produced by artisans, the vast majority of whom were laymen rather than clerics, and all of whom made their living by exercising one of the crafts associated with book production – writing, illumination, miniature painting, and binding. Products of a commercial environment rather than of discerning and individual patronage, the illuminated manuscripts are often of a high level of competence and their production in bulk ranks as among the major achievements of medieval book makers.

The craftsmen involved were not concerned to produce works of artistic originality in the avant-garde styles of the day but to satisfy the demands of a market that largely preferred, as far as the decoration of devotional texts was concerned, competent versions of common images to invention not sanctioned by general usage. There were major stylistic changes, of course, in illumination in the fifteenth century, and these can be followed in the products of the 'top end' of the manuscript book market, to adopt the apt terminology of a recent discussion of the subject, where the taste of the royal court was often a powerful influence.[2] Whereas manuscripts of this kind can be studied by grouping them according to the style and designs used by an outstanding master, and establishing links between one master and another (and even the influence of one manuscript upon another), this approach can lead to a rather mechanical assumption when applied to books like the Playfair Hours that the works of the most able artist were copied by a number of less capable imitators. What we have with the Playfair Hours is a product of the 'middle range' of the market, and we may best study it by identifying the styles and images used in the milieu or 'school' from which it emerged rather than trying to explain its decoration and illustrative cycles by pointing to the direct influence of a prestigeous artist. The images to be found in books like the Playfair Hours – when a customer could afford more than mere marginal decoration and illuminated initial letters – were based on pictures and scenes that probably formed part of the user's visual experience as far as his or her religious life was concerned; the same series of images was liable to be found on altar pieces, walls and hangings in churches, and, by the fifteenth century, could probably be purchased at fairs and from booksellers in the form of woodcuts and engravings.

Although Books of Hours were only one of a number of kinds of book produced by commercial methods in the fifteenth century, they are particularly useful as a source for investigating how book production was organised at the time.[3] This is partly due to the fact that large numbers survive made according to fairly standard models, but also to the fact that liturgical details making up the Use followed in the Hours themselves, that is to say the groups of antiphons, versicles, psalms, hymns and canticles for each of the eight canonical hours of the day, vary from diocese to diocese, so that any particular book is liable to give us some indication of the region for which it was intended. There are exceptions to this: in the fifteenth century the Uses of Paris and Rome were beginning to be followed all over western Europe both by individuals and by members of various religious orders, depriving us of any clue to the intended destination of the Book of Hours in question. Other Uses, however, do provide some kind of pointer.

The text of the Playfair Hours follows the Use of Sarum (the old name for Salisbury), employed only in the Britsh Isles, and indicating that it was intended to be used there. Beyond this, the prefatory calendar with which all Books of Hours begin gives such prominence to Scottish saints that it can only have been designed for someone from Scotland or someone living in Scotland. Similarities of decorative style and pictorial composition between our manuscript and a number of Books of Hours of the Use of Rouen made in that city enable us to be reasonably certain that the Playfair Hours was also made in the Norman capital. This provenance will be supported in the discussion that follows. In the event, the Playfair Hours did not reach Scotland for several centuries after it was made. In the sixteenth century it was in the hands of a French owner, probably in Normandy. It is known that Books of Hours were written and illustrated in great quantities in the Low Countries (especially in Ghent and Bruges) for the English market in the fifteenth century. A large number of such books, of Sarum Use but produced in the Low Countries, survive in Britain, and many of them can be shown to have been there from an early date in their history. Whether northern France made a similar contribution to the book trade in Britain in the fifteenth century is more difficult to establish. The English bought books in Normandy, and in Rouen in particular, when this area was under the control of the kings of England between 1415 and 1450, but in the second half of the fifteenth century it seems that Flanders and the Low Countries were a more important source of supply of illuminated books than northern France. The Playfair Hours and the small number of related manuscripts that will be discussed in conjunction with it, provide examples of exports from Rouen and testify to a trade in books between Normandy and Britain of some proportions, but not such as to rival that with the Low Countries.

A great number of fifteenth century Books of Hours of various French and Flemish Uses are to be found in the British Isles today (just as Sarum Use Books of Hours are to be found in Continental Europe). It would be interesting to know at what time they crossed the Channel northwards, and to discover whether they were brought over by post-medieval antiquarians or whether the fifteenth century bibliophile of London or Edinburgh was happy to own a Book of Hours of, for example, the Use of Rouen (which has certain liturgical similarities with the Sarum Use, such as suffrages after Lauds) if he or she was unable to obtain one of Sarum Use in the preferred style of decoration and illumination. Unfortunately, the evidence which might help to answer this question has not survived: successive rebindings have in many cases removed the fly-leaves on which we might have found the ownership inscriptions that enable us to trace the history of any particular manuscript.

What follows is intended to describe the environment in which the Playfair Hours was produced, and to suggest what sort of questions we should have in mind when looking at books of this kind – this must be the excuse for a rather discursive investigation which aims to see what can be discovered about the people involved in making and selling books in late fifteenth century Rouen as well as examining the manuscript itself. Apart from providing a context, this approach will be seen to have a direct bearing on a number of aspects of the Playfair Hours itself.

2. Rouen in the Late Fifteenth Century

THE Norman capital at this date was a flourishing city, with a population well on the way to the 75,000 souls that it was to achieve by the mid-sixteenth century. François I, king from 1515 to 1547, is said to have described it as the first city in the kingdom, Paris being a region rather than a city. It had received royal support after Louis XI had wrested it from the English in 1449. A bi-annual market with special fiscal privileges had been founded in Caen in 1450 but was moved to Rouen seven years later. Controlling the Seine estuary, Rouen was crucial in supplying the Paris basin with goods and raw materials of all kinds; it was also well positioned to develop links with the industrial centres of northern Europe as well as with Spain and Portugal, the source of many raw materials for its own industries, especially the wool needed for cloth production. Armament production was another significant industry in the city. The opening of fishing grounds in the north Atlantic was to provide a further source of wealth. In all, Rouen's position ensured that it was not only the seat of wealthy merchants and bourgeois families, but also a city with international connections and resident communities of foreign merchants and businessmen.[4]

In 1499, a *Parlement* replaced the Exchequer of Normandy, since 1466 the highest court of the province made up of local nobles and churchmen, and a group of royal judges sent from Paris; the new institution provided a measure of local autonomy and stimulated the formation of a settled lawyer class in the city.[5] There was no university to provide a constant demand for the services of craftsmen associated with book production. The only university in Normandy at this time was at Caen, set up under the English administration of Normandy in 1426; it had among its officials stationers, binders, scribes and illuminators, as did all French universities of the period.[6] Rouen, on the other hand, had a wealthy chapter attached to the cathedral that was prepared to spend large sums of money on keeping its library up to date (capitular accounts of the fifteenth century provide graphic information on the acquisition and repair of books), and there were a number of grammar schools in the city that operated

under the supervision of the chapter.[7] Some archbishops of Rouen were notable bibliophiles. Chief among these was Georges d'Amboise, archbishop from 1499 to 1510; closely involved in royal diplomacy under Louis XII and arbiter of taste at the French court, he had books made in Rouen both by established book producers as well as by the artists whose importation of new Renaissance styles in illumination coincide with the dates of his pontificate.[8]

The significance of all this for our purposes is that Rouen had a mixed population of people who were likely to buy and invest in books. While not rivalling Paris, Rouen remained a major centre of book production in the fifteenth century, especially for Normandy and northern France.

⚜ FIGURE 3 The Annunciation to the Shepherds.
Edinburgh University Library, MS.43, folio 50 verso.

⚜ FIGURE 4 David in Penitence.
Edinburgh University Library, MS.43, folio 55 recto.

3. The Makers of Books

EDIEVAL books very rarely contain any information about the people who made them. The remark in a mid-fifteenth century Book of Hours, of Besançon Use but with Breton saints given prominence, that it was written by one Alan and illuminated by his wife is quite exceptional; while the workshop arrangements it implies may not have been typical (though instances are known where manuscript book producers and dealers worked in partnership with wives who carried on the business after their deaths), it does serve to show that illuminating was not entirely a male-dominated profession.[9]

A number of illuminators whose work has been identified on stylistic grounds have been associated with Rouen, and their presence in the city indicates that scribes and binders were there as well. A celebrated example is the Fastolf Master, whose early work in the style of a major Paris artist of the early fifteenth century, the Master of the Duke of Bedford Hours, has been taken to indicate that he started his career in Paris before undertaking a number of commissions in Rouen in the 1430s and 1440s. He is known to have decorated a Book of Hours of Rouen Use for Jean Garin, a canon of Rouen Cathedral (d.1433), and a book of romances for John Talbot, the Earl of Shrewsbury who played a leading part in the English administration of Normandy in this period. The Fastolf Master seems to have withdrawn across the Channel as the English evacuated Normandy after the fall of Rouen in 1449, since in 1450 he decorated a text of Christine de Pisan for Sir John Fastolf in England. Another anonymous illuminator active in Rouen was that known as the Master of the Geneva Latini, a name taken from the magnificently illuminated copy of Brunetto Latini's *Le Trésor* of *c*.1460 now in Geneva. Among manuscripts associated with this Master are copies of the *Coutumier* of Normandy – no doubt these accounts of local laws were in demand as the area returned to the control of the king of France. At the turn of the century, we have artists such as the Master of Petrarch's Triumphs, one of a number of illuminators who flourished under the aegis of the patronage of Georges d'Amboise and who made up a 'Rouen school' distinguished from indigenous illumination by its quality and by its links with royal and aristocratic patrons; König has recently argued that the origin of this school are to be sought in early sixteenth century Paris and Tours. Even towards the middle of the sixteenth century, illuminated manuscripts of distinction were being produced in the city. The Master of the Ango Hours worked on a manuscript dated 1525 and probably illuminated the cartulary of St Maclou in Rouen in 1531.[10]

Archival sources also make clear that book producers were active in Rouen, though it appears impossible to link any names to surviving books. Incidental references are made to scribes, illuminators and binders in the city from as early as 1264, with mention of a married clerk named Peter as *illustrator*, to the sixteenth century. For our purposes it is probably sufficient to go no later than Stephan Du Moustier, who came from a family closely connected with artistic production – among his immediate relations were goldsmiths – and who was active as an illuminator in Rouen between at least 1502, when he was mentioned among illuminators working for Georges d'Amboise, and 1528; Geoffrey Du Moustier, evidently a near relation, carried on the same craft in the city in 1535.[11]

Some of the people mentioned in available archive sources are described as both illuminator and scribe, but these were two separate crafts. In 1396 Jacquet Du Passeur, an illuminator, was paid 69 *livres* for illuminating and decorating with pictures (*pro illuminando et ymaginando*) a Pontifical for the archbishop, whereas the scribe, Guillaume De La Rue, received a separate payment of 36 *livres* for writing the text and supplying the parchment. Scribes did not only write books. Cathedral accounts show a number of scribes being paid 7 *livres* and 10 *sous* in 1466 for writing 700 *brevets*, probably indulgences and notices of various kinds sent to parishes in the diocese, while in 1475 a single scribe, Nicole Heulté, received 6 *livres* and 5 *sous* (and 35 *sous* for parchment) for 500 *brevets*. A scribe named Guillebert Pouchet supplied most of the cathedral's needs for this kind of document in the late fifteenth century, and the numbers involved show clearly that scribes could produce texts in bulk: in 1488 he supplied 1152 *brevets* to be sent '*aux curés du diocese de Rouen*', though some of this work may have been subcontracted. After this date, public notices and indulgences were usually supplied in lots of 1000 by printers. Scribes of this kind might have a legal background – Guillaume Dombreville and Ernaud Billon, paid in 1469 for supplying 577 *brevets*, were '*notaires en cour d'église*' – or even be clerics: Guillebert Pouchet was a priest. It is known that an Augustinian canon, Jehan Langloys, earned his living as a scribe immediately after 1500, but the source that reveals this also mentions laymen paid for writing constituent parts of books: Breton Raulet, Michel Leroux, Pierre Boyvin and Étienne de Vaulx. Scribes of this kind also made money by teaching: in 1492 it was found necessary to prohibit writing masters from putting advertisements (*'écriteaux pro introductione artis scribendi'*) on the cathedral door.[12]

Though the crafts of writing and illuminating could be exercised by a single individual, references in fifteenth century accounts of Rouen churches such as St Nicholas de Rouen or the cathedral show payments being made to illuminators, scribes and binders as separate categories of craftsmen. A register from the municipal archives of Rouen refers incidentally to four men described as illuminators in May 1484; the fact that three of them, Jean Masselin, Jean Le Moigne and Guillaume Coutil lived in the parish of Sainte Croixe – Saint Ouen, while another, Guillaume Longuet, lived nearby, near the Dominican convent, suggests that people engaged in the same craft lived in the same part of the city. In this case, all the addresses are near the *Place du Vieux Marché*, some distance to the west of the cathedral, where in 1431 Joan of Arc was finally declared an excommunicate and handed over to the secular power for execution. It is particularly unfortunate that these people cannot be linked with any of the numerous books assigned to late fifteenth century Rouen, especially since the Playfair Hours can be assigned to roughly this period.[13]

Despite this evidence for the activities of book producers in Rouen, there appears to be no indication of any guild or confraternity that grouped together those involved in making books. After the recovery of Rouen in 1449, the French royal *bailli* appointed to administer the city produced a series of statutes for a number of guilds, from barbers and milliners to armament makers and cloth workers.[14] Whereas in Paris the *Confrérie des Libraires, Écrivains, Enlumineurs, Parcheminiers et Relieurs de Livres* had its statutes proclaimed by royal decree in 1467, there appears to have been no equivalent in Rouen.[15] Parchment makers of the city belonged to the leatherworkers guild, whose privileges were confirmed in 1492, but it is not until 1557 that reference can be found to a guild designed to protect the interests and regulate the work of book producers, the Corporation of Printers and Booksellers. Such a guild may have existed prior to this, since a description of the pageantry that accompanied the entry of Henri II into Rouen in 1550 refers to booksellers and parchment makers as two distinct groups among the trades represented.[16]

4. *The Book Trade*

How did people set about acquiring books in fifteenth century Rouen? Who was responsible for organising their production and meeting the requirements of customers? Though our sources do not allow us to give very precise answers to these questions, they do enable us to observe certain aspects of the book trade at the time the Playfair Hours was produced, some of which will be of relevance when we consider this manuscript closely.

It is apparent from what has been said above that the church provided a great deal of work for book producers. Apart from keeping service books in good condition and seeing that additions and alterations were made as liturgical practices changed, the cathedral also saw that parish churches had books necessary for services: in 1391 the canons had a Missal made for the church at Manneville-la-Goupil for 40 gold francs, while in 1420 they made a contribution of 4 *livres* towards the 9 *livres* needed by the Martin Église parish church for a new Missal, evidently a less expensive affair. This sort of activity carried on right through the century. In 1497 the canons supplied parish churches with printed Missals. In most of these cases, recourse was had directly to the craftsmen concerned, though the work might also be done by applying to a bookseller. On 13 December 1400, a bookseller by the name of Jean Le Queue undertook to supply the Convent of St. Jacques with an illuminated Missal for 40 *livres* in circumstances which show that he would ensure that the work was done rather than do it himself. Jean Coquet, termed *libraire*, saw to the rebinding of books of St Nicolas de Rouen in 1469, and also sold the church a ready-made book, a Processionary, some years later.[17]

The rôle of booksellers will be discussed below, but it is worth pointing out how one section of society arranged for books to be made according to its taste. William Bradwardine, Lord of St Vaast and La Poterie, hired Jacquet Le Caron, a native of Châtel-la-Lune near Rouen, in March 1420 to exercise his craft as

✤ FIGURE 5 The Presentation of Christ at the Temple.
Cambridge University Library, Add.MS.4099, folio 60 recto.

scribe and illuminator (*'métier d'écrire et enluminer'*) for one year at a salary of 20 *livres*. This was probably quite a high salary: a century later servants in Rouen could expect to earn 8 *livres* a year. Bradwardine was to lodge, clothe and feed his servant, provide him with a workshop (*hostel*), and buy all the materials (*estoffes*) that he needed for his work. What we see here is an illuminator joining a minor aristocratic household, and one may speculate that the patron had some kind of say in the kind of decoration produced by his servant.[18]

This solution to the problem of getting books was confined to the wealthy and powerful. Most people relied on *libraires*, also called *libratiers*, that is to say booksellers, to obtain the books they wanted, and it is clear that people of this description were at the centre of a flourishing book trade throughout the fifteenth century.

There is a reference in 1400 to a *libratier* 'of the parish of St Laurent' to the north west of the cathedral; given the fact that a grammar school was situated in the parish, it may be that he carried on his business there.[19] However, it is plain for most of the fifteenth century that the area immediately to the north of the cathedral was the centre of the book trade, as, indeed, it is today. In April 1418, the chapter bought a breviary from one Jean Boyvin, a book seller (*marchand de livres*) at the *Portail des Boursiers* on the north side of the cathedral. In 1456, the Master of Works of the cathedral had to discuss his plans for repairing the cathedral fabric with the *'libraires qui tiennent échoppes au Portail des Boursiers'*. On 1 October 1468 the canons forbade the booksellers of the *Portail Nord* to open their shops (*boutiques*) on that day since it was the Feast of the Dedication of the Cathedral. By 1479, this entrance was being called the *Portail des Libraires*, possibly a change in name resulting from the expansion of business in selling books. On 13 September 1481 a commission was appointed to advise on the construction of an entrance at this spot, 'where the booksellers now have their shops', that would do honour to the church. From 1487, accounts survive of rents paid by booksellers at the *Portail des Libraires* to the cathedral chapter for their premises. Books were also sold in the square in front of the cathedral, some by people like Gaillat Le Bourgeois, who already had shops at the *Portail des Libraires*, and some by traders whose business may have been

⚜ FIGURE 6 The Nativity.
Bodleian Library, Oxford, MS. Douce 253, folio 50 recto.

24

more freelance and itinerant in character. On 5 July 1482 a tradesman described as a *mercier* was forbidden to sell *papiros seu libellos* at the *Grand Portail*, that is to say in front of the cathedral, but the principle was admitted that books of a respectable nature could be sold there once a licence had been acquired from the Master of the Works, a principle confirmed the following year. From 1489, accounts survive that show the chapter taking rents for stalls (*estal*) mounted by booksellers at the main door of the cathedral. As an economic and social centre, the cathedral attracted tradesmen such as booksellers: in 1488, such people were doing business at another cathedral entrance, that of the *Portail St Romain*, but on 30 October of that year they were ordered to confine themselves to the *Portail des Libraires*.[20]

Where else in Rouen were books sold? The presence of illuminators around the old market, mentioned above, suggests that this may have been another centre of the book trade. In the sixteenth century it is clear that booksellers were also established around the *Palais de Justice*; whether this was the case before 1500 does not appear.[21]

The chief activity of the *libraire* was the selling of books. Many came from families that were closely involved in book production. The *libraire* Jean Coquet who saw to the repair of an Epistolary of St Nicolas de Rouen in 1447 had relatives named Colin Coquet and Michaut Coquet – their work as binders is mentioned in the archives of the same abbey between 1439 and 1469. The *libraire* Jean Boyvin mentioned in 1418 had a relation named Jean Boyvin, described as an illuminator in 1440. The widow of one Thomas Boyvin, *libraire*, was running a bookshop at the *Porte des Libraires* in 1487; Pierre Boyvin, a priest, is referred to as an illuminator in 1502, and a Robert Boyvin in 1534–1542 worked at the same trade, supplying 'vignettes' (miniatures) for books at 30 *sous* each (he also painted separate pictures '*en or et azur*' on parchment to be placed in reliquaries).[22] Whether or not any bookseller actually exercised a craft associated with book production, the major part of his activities was entrepreneurial, seeing that orders were taken and stock maintained, schedules of production met, and generally acting as 'middleman' between customer and the various craftsmen who provided parchment, wrote the text, illuminated the folios and bound the finished product. That the

⚜ FIGURE 7 The Nativity.
Cambridge University Library, Add.MS.4099, folio 50 recto.

eus in adiutorium
meum intende.
Domine ad ad
iuuandum me festina.

activity of a *libraire* was seen as a craft in its own right and not as an incidental activity carried out by a binder or illuminator is shown in the sixteenth century by the guild that they organised. In late fifteenth century Paris, where the activities of University *libraires* can be traced back to the thirteenth century, we have a reference to an apprentice *libraire* in 1488, evidently learning the trade from one of the official *libraires* authorised by the university.[23]

The rôle of the *libraire* Jean Le Queue, mentioned earlier in connection with a transaction of 1400, is seen clearly in a contract made by him in 1394, when one Gérard Jumier, then living in Rouen, undertook to work for him as an illuminator for one year at a salary of 15 *livres* with board and lodging. Such arrangements may have been common. No such contract has yet been discovered for late fifteenth century Rouen, and indeed this is not the kind of private transaction of which details are likely to survive. However, an agreement of identical tenor survives for Avignon, where on 5 April 1481 a *libraire* by the name of Joachim of Rome took into his service a binder-scribe-illuminator called Jean Donat; payment was by the amount of work done, and Donat was allowed to write prayer books, 'alphabets' and Psalters to sell on his own account.[24]

Though a bookseller might have some work carried out on his own premises, it is likely that much if not most of it was contracted out to other individuals. This may go some way towards explaining why so many fifteenth century Rouen Books of Hours contain the work of a number of artists. In the case of the Playfair Hours, there appears to be the work of seven separate hands or styles for the illumination, some of them confined to individual gatherings. This will be discussed later, but the physical aspects of the manuscript do support the notion of booksellers acting as entrepreneurs co-ordinating the activities of craftsmen.

What sort of stock did booksellers keep in fifteenth century Rouen? To suggest that they had woodcuts, engravings and devotional paintings, the latter produced by the same methods as a folio from a manuscript book, is pure speculation. The fact that painters and 'makers of images' (probably pictures) were allowed to sell their wares in the cathedral ambulatory in 1459, provided

⚜ FIGURE 8 The Nativity.
National Library of Scotland, MS.6131, folio 26 verso.

28

Deus in adiutorium meum in
tende. [Domi]ne ad adiuuandum
me festina. Gloria patri et
filio et spiritui sancto. Sicut erat in prin
cipio et nunc et semper et in secula seculorum
Amen. Hymnus

they were decent, does not rule out this possibility. Given the familiarity with involved financial dealing that bookselling implies, it may be that booksellers were also dealers in writing and illuminating materials for other craftsmen. The totally chance survival of information about the estate of a Paris bookseller who died in 1475, a *libraire-juré* of the University, shows that he had expensive equipment for grinding pigments, which lays open the possibility that he had a store of it for sale or for those to whom he passed texts for decoration on behalf of customers – he also had '*pourtraitures, des histoires et des vignettes*', probably models for illumination, which might also have been used in this way. This particular bookseller is known to have had second hand books in his stock, and it is likely that the same was true of Rouen booksellers. To whom else but local booksellers would the chapter sell off unwanted volumes from the cathedral library, as it did throughout the fifteenth century? On one occasion, in 1465, it was decided to send a number of such books to Paris to be exchanged for others (a useful reminder both of the extent of book trading, which was more than purely local, and the dominant position of Paris where the supply of books was concerned), but in most cases it is difficult not to assume that Rouen book-sellers acquired them. The sums of money involved were considerable. Books described as *inutiles et anciens* were sold for 79 *livres* in 1459; in 1465 it was decided to sell two books to help pay for repairs to the fabric: if these books were anything like the copy of Gratian's *Decretum* which fetched 55 *livres* in 1468 or the canon law text known as the *Clementinae*, sold for 10 *écus d'or* (i.e. 30 *livres*) at the same date, then the sum gained was considerable. But apart from these academic text books, we would probably not be far wrong if we assumed that a bookseller would also have in stock the literary texts, romances, astrological works and, of course, Books of Hours, that were sought by the reading public of the day.[25]

By the date that the Playfair Hours was produced, booksellers would also have had in their stock a number of printed texts. It is worth saying something on the subject of early printing in Rouen, since it both throws light on the activities of the booksellers in the city and also provides evidence of a pattern of trade which will be directly relevant to our consideration of the Playfair Hours itself.

Printing was introduced into Paris in 1470, but it was not until 1486 that Antoine Vérard produced a Books of Hours. Given the market for such things, this delay may imply that demand was being tolerably well met by manuscript book producers and that the crucial factor that made Books of Hours marketable was their decorative aspects which printing at this time had no pretensions to rival. The first Book of Hours of Rouen Use was produced in Paris by Vérard in *c.*1488, though printed Books of Hours of Paris or Rome Use may have been saleable in the Norman capital before this.

Printed books were being sold in Rouen in the 1480s, and it appears that their arrival had a somewhat dislocating effect on the established trade. It is likely that the *mercier* mentioned above who in 1482 was forbidden to sell *papiros seu libellos* was dealing with printed items, since the words used to describe his wares were not those used to describe hand-written codices. We learn from capitular decisions of 5 and 7 July 1483 that the Rouen *libraires* had banded together in an effort to expel people who were selling printed books on the *parvis* in front of the cathedral. In the event, the chapter decided not to drive out these salesmen provided that they sold only *libros peroptimos et utiles*. Printed books were specifically mentioned in this case. When the established booksellers complained in January 1487 and November 1488 that 'foreign' booksellers were leaving chests of their books overnight in the cathedral, these books were not described; the sudden rash of complaints does however suggest that these 'foreigners' had different kinds of wares, probably cheaper in price than the traditional hand-written book. The Chapter had no objection to these newcomers, provided that they bought licences to carry on their trade – the provision was repeatedly made that nothing indecent was to be offered for sale. In all, the arrival of printing in Rouen can be compared to that of the video-cassette today, with all its implications for the established film industry.[26]

Among the first to invest in the new technology of printing in Rouen were, not surprisingly, the families of the wealthier booksellers. Guillaume Le Talleur, thought to have been responsible for the earliest printing in the city with an account of Charles VII's entry in 1485, was son of a burgher of Rouen – it has been argued that he learnt the art of printing in Paris with Jean Du Pré, among whose productions was a *Coutumier de Normandie* of 1483 designed for the Norman market.[27] The second Rouen printer was Jean Le Bourgeois, no doubt a close relation of Gaillat Le Bourgeois who in the late 1480s paid rent for two bookshops, at the *Portail des Libraires* and at the *Grand Portail* of the cathedral. It was in the *'hostel'* of Gaillat Le Bourgeois that Jean Le Bourgeois printed his first dated work, a text of *Launcelot du Lac*, in November 1488. In 1498 Jean Le Bourgeois was described as a *libraire*; he was probably the same man as printed in Rouen in that year a commentary on Aristotle for a Caen bookseller, Robert Macé. Another case where an early Rouen printer can be shown to have been related to booksellers is that of Jacques Le Forestier, whose earliest dated printing was done in the city in 1494. He was evidently from the family of Gaillat Le Forestier and Michel Le Forestier, both known to have been booksellers at this time.[28]

In the 1480s, Rouen became the centre of printing in Normandy – the earliest printing in the province had been in 1480 at Caen, but after the production of one book, presses are not recorded there until the late 1490s, and Rouen printers supplied the needs of Caen booksellers.[29]

Printers in Rouen also produced books for the English market, and while not matching the bulk of imports from the Low Countries and Germany, became a significant source of supply. It has been convincingly demonstrated that one of the first Sarum Use Books of Hours to have been printed, in 1495, was the work of a Rouen printing press, that of Jacques Le Forestier.[30] Missals, Breviaries, Manuals and other liturgical books of Sarum Use were printed in the city for the British market. Martin Morin produced three editions of the Sarum Missal and two of the Sarum Breviary between 1492 and 1500 for export from Rouen, at least some of them through the agency of Jean Richard, a bookseller of Rouen who appears to have been in charge of the French side of an operation involving booksellers from the British Isles. Richard Pynson, a Norman by birth who took over William de Machlinia's business as a printer and seller of law books in London in c.1490, had a number of English law books printed in Rouen by Guillaume Le Talleur.[31] Books such as the Playfair Hours, together with other Rouen manuscripts made for use in Scotland such as MS.43 in Edinburgh University Library, the Yester Hours in Magdalene College, Cambridge, and the Farmor Hours in The Hague, show that the trade in printed books followed a pattern of trade established by manuscript books.[32]

The British market was only part of that served by Rouen book producers, of course. A Book of Hours of the Use of Le Mans illuminated in Rouen in c.1470 serves as an example of a manuscript book made for sale beyond Normandy, just as the *Coutumier de Bretagne* printed in Rouen by Martin Morin in 1492 shows the same activity continuing with the new technology.[33]

⚜ FIGURE 9 The Nativity.
Bodleian Library, Oxford, MS. Buchanan e 3, folio 29 recto.

Booksellers in Rouen evidently developed their entrepreneurial skills in dealing with manuscript books and adapted swiftly to the new technology. Before the end of the fifteenth century we find them arranging for the printing of books on behalf of booksellers in other towns, and having works printed for themselves on presses in other places such as Paris. The pattern would be familiar to any twentieth century publisher. Whether before the advent of printing Rouen booksellers had texts written out for them by scribes from outside the city is not known. A fifteenth century binding done in Paris contains an 'open' and uncut piece of parchment on which is the text of four folios of a Books of Hours, that is to say that it was discarded from a scribe's workshop before it had been folded horizontally and vertically and cut to make two independent *bifolia*. The text is rare – the Hours of the Holy Sacrament and the Hours of St Katherine – but the hymn used for Prime shows that the Use of Rouen was being followed, allowing us to speculate that we see the work of a Paris scribe producing a text to be sold, and possibly even illuminated, in Rouen.[35] It is known that one Paris bookseller in the late fifteenth century had a scribe working for him at a considerable distance from the city, so that he had to correspond by letter and transfer texts by a messenger, but the *'lieu plaisant'* where the scribe resided is not mentioned. If there was some kind of trade in texts and incomplete (and unbound) manuscript books, it is not likely to have been of significant proportions. The swift circulation of early printed texts in an incomplete state (un-illuminated and unbound), like that of the celebrated Gutenberg Bible, distributed widely and quickly in the 1450s and illuminated in the style of the place where it was sold, argues for a well developed book trade, but it appears impossible to know if such texts had manuscript precursors.[36]

5. *The Playfair Hours: The History of the Manuscript*

THE Playfair Hours was given to the Library of the Victoria and Albert Museum in 1918 by Sir Otto Beit, who had bought it from the Reverend Dr Patrick M. Playfair of St Andrews – the latter had offered it for sale for the benefit of the Scottish Red Cross on condition that it should become national property.[37] Members of the Playfair family remembered at the time of the transaction that the volume had been in the family's possession in *c.*1835–1845. The manuscript was certainly in either England or Scotland in the early nineteenth century. The volume was then rebound, and the decorative tooling on the spine shows that this was done in England in *c.*1820 or a little earlier.[38] This is the first indication that the volume had left Normandy. A note on the fly-leaf of the binding in an eighteenth century French hand, 'Lemiere, 8[*or* s].1.d', may either have been made by a bookseller or an owner. Also written on the fly-leaf is a poem written in cipher (with a transliteration in an eighteenth century hand) which is dated 1564 and reveals that the volume then belonged to 'Dame Charlotte'. The poem refers to the 'excellente couverture', probably to be identified with the boards, retained in the nineteenth century binding, which are French and datable to *c.*1550–1560.[39] There are also roughly painted coats of arms on the fly-leaves and the last folio; these may be later than the sixteenth century, or done at that period by a decidedly amateur hand. The arms in question are not specific enough to be attributed to any family.[40]

Ownership of the volume cannot be traced back further than this, but enough has been said to show that it remained in France until some time before *c.*1820. The manuscript's history differs from other books made in Rouen for Scottish customers. The Book of Hours now in Magdalen College, Cambridge, the 'Yester Hours', records the death of John, Lord Hay of Yester, in 1508; it was owned by John Laflyn of That Ilk later in the sixteenth century.[41] The Book of Hours now in The Hague, the 'Farmor Hours', was owned by 'George Farmor', according to an inscription in an italic hand on the fly-leaf.[42] Inscriptions in different hands enable this person to be identified as belonging

to the Farmor family of Easton Neston, Northamptonshire, from which one Mary married Robert Crichton, Lord Sanquhar, in London in 1604 and, after Sanquhar's execution in 1612, Barnaby O'Brien, Earl of Thomond in 1615. The reference to Sanquhar provides a link with Scotland – he was a Roman Catholic active in the service of the king of Scotland in the late sixteenth century – but it is impossible to say whether the manuscript came into the Farmor family through him, since there is no means of knowing if the George Farmor mentioned above was the person of this name whose marriage to Mary Curzon in 1572 was noted on folio 148v of the manuscript, or his son of the same name who noted the death of his own second son Robert Farmor at Carlow in Ireland in 1616 and details of his sister Mary's delivery of a son to her second husband in 1617.

The fact that the Playfair Hours did not come to Scotland early in its history does not mean that we have to exclude it from the group of manuscripts which we know were designed for, and being used in, the British Isles in the sixteenth century. For the Farmor Hours, its presence there might be deduced also by the fact that the word 'pope' has been scraped away wherever it appeared in the calendar, though oddly enough the feast of St Thomas a Becket of Canterbury on 29 December has been left intact (suppressed by Henry VIII, it is very often found erased in Books of Hours in England and Scotland that survived the Reformation). Since the feast of Pope Silvester on 30 December has also been left untouched, it may be that the owner of the manuscript tired of correcting the book before he or she reached this point.

FIGURE 10 Cover (French, mid-sixteenth century) and spine (English, *c*.1820 or slightly earlier) of the binding of the Playfair Hours.

⚜ FIGURE 11 The Adoration of the Magi.
Cambridge University Library, Add.MS.4099, folio 57 verso.

6. *The Structure and Text of the Playfair Hours*

OUR manuscript provides a particularly full version of prayers current in late fifteenth century France and Britain, quite apart from a standard version of the Hours of the Virgin Mary. Only four leaves are missing from the volume. Two of them, with the beginning of the Seven Joys of the Virgin and the first of the suffrages to the saints (between folios 26–27 and 171–172 respectively) very probably contained miniatures. The third missing folio, containing part of a prayer to Christ (between folios 183–184) and the fourth, with the last part of the prayer on Christ's Seven Last Words and the beginning of St John's account of the Passion (between folios 195–196) may also have done; they can only be discerned by a break in the text. These excisions may all have been made in the nineteenth century at the time of the Victorian vogue for making collections of illumination cut from medieval books.[43]

The script used in the Playfair Hours is that known as *lettre bâtarde*, frequently met with in Books of Hours and in literary or historical texts. Though it is possible that a single scribe wrote out the different parts of the manuscript, we may be misled by the expertise of scribes in the fifteenth century who could produce such consistent versions of common hands that it sometimes appears impossible to identify the script of an individual. It may be that differences in the colour of the ink show different hands at work, or at least different stints of work on the part of a single scribe. The gatherings (i.e. the booklets made up of a number of *bifolia*) that contain the Hours themselves (folios 36–79) are in a consistent brown ink, while the gatherings containing the Psalter of St Jerome and the Verses of St Bernard (folios 152–167) are in a uniform black ink that contrasts with that, light brown, on the preceding and following gatherings.

Apart from the calendar, discussed below, the text is written on regular gatherings of four *bifolia*, that is to say booklets of eight folios. The regularity is not totally consistent, as can be seen from the collation given with the technical description of the manuscript, but it does reveal a standardised format evidencing the 'mass-produced' nature of such books. Some parts of the text are confined to particular gatherings or groups of gatherings and can thus be regarded as separate 'units of production'. Apart from the calendar, the Hours of the Virgin Mary, for instance, are written on six separate gatherings, five of 8 folios and one of 4 folios (folios 36–79). Another part of the text confined to particular gatherings is the Psalter of St Jerome and succeeding matter, mentioned above as written in black ink. Identification of such units within the manuscript is important, since each gathering may have had a separate history before being bound together, for instance being passed to a different artist for miniature painting.

The text itself begins with the Gospel sequences, after which is a very full set of prayers prefacing the Hours of the Virgin Mary.[44] Apart from the usual prayers *Obsecro te*, said to have been composed by St Augustine and containing a plea for a vision of the Virgin on the reader's deathbed, and *O Intemerata*, a prayer traced back to the twelfth century and thought to have originated in a Cistercian abbey, the Playfair Hours includes the Seven Joys of the Virgin (Annunciation, Nativity, Presentation at the Temple, Epiphany, Birth of Christ, Resurrection, Ascension) often said, as here, to have been composed by St Thomas a Becket, followed by the Five Corporeal Joys of the Virgin and a prayer beginning *O illustrissima et excellentissima gloriosa semper virgo Maria* which is found in a number of early sixteenth century French Books of Hours.

After the Hours of the Virgin Mary, with the Hours of the Cross at the end of each, come other essential prayers that make up books of this kind: Penitential Psalms, Litany and Office of the Dead, with the noteworthy addition of the Gradual Psalms, thought to have been developed by the Carolingian monastic reformer, St Benedict of Aniane, in the early ninth century, and the Psalms of the Passion. Prayers to the Holy Sacrament of the Altar and to the Trinity are followed by the Psalter of St Jerome, an abbreviated version of the Psalter made up of single verses taken from different Psalms and designed for use by those who had insufficient time to recite the complete Psalter. Psalms too are the basis of the Verses of St Bernard that follow, again made up of verses from different Psalms. A profusion of suffrages to saints and prayers to Christ, followed by the prayer on the Seven Last Words of Christ on the Cross, often attributed to the Venerable Bede, and St John's account of Christ's Passion (chapters XVIII & XIX) bring the text to a close.

✤ FIGURE 12　The Adoration of the Magi.
Bodleian Library, Oxford, MS. Douce 253, folio 58 recto.

✢ FIGURE 13 The Adoration of the Magi.
Bodleian Library, Oxford, MS. Douce 72, folio 36 recto.

42

7. The Calendar of the Playfair Hours

NOTHING in the text of the Playfair Hours thus far deviates from standard versions of the Sarum Use. Scottish saints such as Columban appear in the Litany, but this is a regular feature of all Sarum Litanies. The distinctive part of the text which shows unequivocally that it was intended for a Scottish user is the calendar, with which all Books of Hours begin. It was written on a single gathering of 6 *bifolia*, with entries alternatively in blue and red but with major feasts in gold. That it was a separate 'unit of production' is shown by the fact that the hand is of a slightly different kind from that of the body of the text.

Of the major feasts in the calendar that are written in gold, all but two are standard in the Sarum calendar. The exceptions are the feast of St Kentigern (d.612), the patron saint of Glasgow, on 13 January, and the feast of St Ninian, the reputed apostle of the Picts in the fifth century, on 16 September. These two feasts are also in gold in the Farmor Hours. The former is also a major feast in EUL 43 and Yester Hours, though the latter is a simple feast in both; all four calendars include the translation of St Ninian as an ordinary feast on 31 August. Other Scottish saints in the Playfair Hours are St Fillan of Strathfillan, Perthshire, an eighth century saint to whom the Scottish army of Robert the Bruce attributed its victory at Bannockburn in 1314, on 9 January; St Monan, the Evangelist of Fife who, according to the Aberdeen Breviary of 1510, came to Scotland from Pannonia in Hungary with St Adrian, on 1 March; St Adrian himself (d.875), of the Ile of May, on 4 March; St Baldred, a suffragan of Kentigern who became a hermit on the latter's death and whose feast was also celebrated at Durham, on 6 March; the Cornish St Constantine, another associate of Kentigern who according to one tradition was martyred at Kintyre in 576, on 9 March; and St Kessog of Luss, Dumbarton, a sixth century saint martyred in 560 on the banks of Loch Lomond.

These saints all have associations with the southern parts of Scotland, Kentigern and Ninian being linked closely with the Glasgow and Galloway area. The Scottish saints are celebrated on the same days in the calendars of EUL 43, the Yester Hours and the Farmor Hours, though Kessog appears only in the Playfair Hours; Monan appears solely in the Playfair Hours and in the Farmor Hours. The calendars of EUL 43 and the Yester Hours are identical – what differences there are can be explained by scribal error. The Farmor Hours is closer to the Playfair Hours, and usually follows the latter when it deviates from EUL 43 and Yester Hours. However, it is clear that the Farmor calendar was an independent compilation from that of the Playfair Hours, being alone in giving a bishop *Colmatus* for 13 March and *Hippolitus* and his companions for 12 August, and preferring bishop *Iuvenalis*, like EUL 43 and the Yester Hours, for the Playfair Hours' *Donatus* on 21 May.

It is fairly common for calendars in books like the Playfair Hours to contain mistakes. No doubt they crept into the manuscript tradition as successive copies of a model were made. Thus we have '*Gaciani episcopi*' on 18 December for *Gratiani episcopi*. The two other manuscripts, EUL 43 and the Yester Hours avoid this mistake, but the three do share a number of others, showing that they derive from the same family group of texts: '*Maturini*' for *Marini* on 3 March, '*Maximiani*' for *Martiniani* on 5 May, and '*Severini*' for *Servatii* on 13 May (the Farmor Hours has no entries for these dates). The four calendars share what appear to be errors of date for feasts, or at least an eccentric observance. Pope *Cletus* or Anacletus is celebrated on 7 May rather than on the more usual 26 April, while the feast of '*Domiciani*', more properly *Donatiani* (Donation, bishop of Reims) is commonly found on 14 October rather than 6 September, as here. In one instance, the scribe of the Playfair Hours calendar has misplaced the feast by one day, putting *Donatus* on 21 May rather than the correct 22 May: the reason for this may be that the scribe wanted to keep a regular layout on the page and to fill in the gap between the major feast of St Dunstan on 19 May and *Desiderius* on 23 May with an entry mid-way between them rather than leaving two lines empty after Dunstan's entry. The three other calendars are no help here, since they have bishop '*Inverialis*' on 21 May, probably a misspelling for *Iuvenalis* which only the scribe of the Farmor Hours avoided. The scribe of the latter manuscript gives Dunstan as '*Dunastanus*' – one may picture a French scribe struggling with foreign names. It is worth noticing that the scribe just mentioned appears to have made a similar mistake to that in the Playfair Hours just mentioned: the three other calendars have *Justinus*, *Marcellus* and *Erasmus* (spelt '*Hersinus*' by the Playfair Hours scribe) for the first, second and third feasts of June, whereas the Farmor Hours omits the first name, having *Marcellus* and *Erasmus* for the first and second of this month.

44

These comments on the accuracy of the calendar rather undermine its use as a source for examining the development of devotions in the late medieval period. They also reduce the value of the slight clues that it contains as regards dating. The calendars of religious houses, cathedrals and other churches, can include elements that provide some indication of the date at which they were drawn up, for instance including a feast which is known to have been propagated by papal or provincial decree at a particular date. The Transfiguration appears as an ordinary feast in the calendar of the Playfair Hours on 6 August. This feast had been celebrated by a number of religious orders in the fourteenth century, but was promulgated by a papal bull of 1457 which recommended that it be commemorated as a double feast on that day; in England it seems to have been adopted in the late 1480s, and only by 1495 was it fully integrated into the Sarum Use. This would argue for a late date for the Playfair Hours, i.e. c.1480–1490, were it not for the fact that the whole calendar was made up in Rouen where the feast appears in the liturgy in the fourteenth century and figures fairly consistently in the calendar after 1457, being promulgated in 1468 and made *triplex* in 1474. The feast of the Transfiguration may thus have got into the calendar along with a number of other Rouen feasts (e.g. St Ausbert, archbishop, on 9 February; St Hugh, archbishop, on 9 March; St Mellon, archbishop, on 22 October; and, above all, St Romain, archbishop, on 23 October) rather than representing Sarum usage proper.[45]

However, we are perhaps on surer ground with other feasts that appear in our calendar. The feast of the Visitation on 2 July, a major feast, was promulgated at the Council of Basel in 1441, and is found here and there in French service books thereafter, but it was only after the promulgation of the feast by Sixtus IV in 1475 that it began to gain general observance. A feast which begins to appear in Sarum calendars from the 1490s is that of the Crown of Thorns, entered in our calendar on 4 May; the fact that it occurs chiefly in printed mass books, a good number of them printed abroad, may argue for a continental origin. The evidence for dating is therefore somewhat ambiguous. What we have with the Playfair Hours is a calendar 'cobbled together' in Rouen using a version of the Sarum calendar interspersed with Scottish feasts and with an admixture of feasts from Rouen and northern France generally. It is worth noticing that the calendars of the Yester and Farmor Hours, as well as EUL 43, agree with the Playfair calendar in making the Visitation on 2 July a major feast and that all include the Transfiguration and Crown of Thorns as ordinary feasts, with the exception of the Farmor Hours where these two dates are both left blank. From the negative point of view, none of these calendars include the feast of the Name of Christ (*Nomen Christi*) for 7 August, which appears regularly in the calendars of printed Books of Hours of Sarum Use from 1495 and which begins to enter Sarum calendars generally from about this date.[46]

8. *Illumination: The Calendar*

IF the text of the calendar indicates an intended Scottish owner, the decoration of this part of the manuscript provides compelling evidence that it was made in Rouen. The series of pictures showing the labours of the month (plates I–VIII) and signs of the zodiac come from a set that was commonly used in Books of Hours of Rouen Use, as well as in EUL 43 and the Yester Hours.

In the Playfair Hours we find these pictures used to fill almost half of the area ruled for writing on the recto of each folio. In other manuscripts they usually appear in an abbreviated version, confined to a rectangular compartment in the middle of the right-hand margin, and featuring two figures, or even one, to the Playfair Hours' three. Naturally enough, the scene is generally set in a more confined space when it appears in the margin, though the figures are more or less the same size. It is the abbreviated version of the labour of the month pictures that appears in EUL 43 (figure 14) and the Yester Hours, in both of which the border decoration is in the same style as that of the Playfair Hours: blue and brushed gold acanthus leaves interspersed with sprays of berries, fruit and flowers, stylised but sufficiently realistic for some species to be recognised, together with compartments of these same sprays on a brushed gold ground.

Exactly the same set of calendar illustrations is to be found in a Rouen Use Book of Hours now in Cambridge (CUL Add.4099); this has the same border decoration as the two manuscripts just mentioned, though lacking the compartments of brushed gold.

Though the backgrounds to this series of pictures vary – a landscape of wooded slopes and distant blue hills surmounted by towers, found in the Playfair Hours, might be exchanged for an interior with a simple grey wall behind the figures or a hanging of red brocade – the dress, position of the figures, the costume, and on occasion the colouring of the garments, are all

⚜ FIGURE 14 Calendar illustrations for January and December. Edinburgh University Library, MS.43, folios 1 recto and 12 recto.

🏵 FIGURE 15 Calendar illustrations for January and December.
Edinburgh University Library, MS.306, folios 1 recto and 12 recto.

48

extremely close, though executed in a more or less finished manner. Differences of this kind may indicate that the same set of drawings was being used by a number of different craftsmen within a workshop or in separate workshops.

These calendar pictures had a long history in Rouen book production, and systematic search for them would probably enable us to follow it more closely than we can here. A Book of Hours of Rouen Use now in Edinburgh, E U L 306 (figure 15), has the same series of pictures to decorate its calendar, rather more crudely executed than in the Playfair Hours and reducing the scene to a single figure where it can. The marginal decoration here consists of large sprays of rather less stylised flowers – roses and pansies can be identified – and multi-coloured acanthus leaves, the whole on a ground of brushed gold; we may not greatly err in dating this manuscript to the end of the fifteenth century, possibly the last decade.

The same pictures are to be found in another Book of Hours of Rouen Use now in the National Library of Scotland (NLS 6129). This manuscript has a slightly different border decoration, multicoloured acanthus leaves and sprays of stylised fruit and flowers, the whole on a brushed gold ground; a number of features argue for a slightly later date than the group associated with the Playfair Hours mentioned earlier. The scene of the Annunciation in this manuscript (figure 26) has an architectural frame consisting of an elaborate classical arch with Corinthian capitals, fluted columns, and cherubs at each extremity of the triangular pediment. These features of Renaissance style would date the manuscript to about the first decade of the sixteenth century, and indeed may show a reaction on the part of the makers of 'middle range of the market' manuscripts in Rouen to the styles of artists working for Georges d'Amboise in the city.

Rather later in date is Douce 72 in the Bodleian Library. The calendar here (figure 16) is written in a small script, a version of *lettre bâtarde*, in two columns, above each of which is a picture of the labour of the month and the appropriate zodiac sign side by side. The calendar pictures are neatly and simply executed, the scenes being shown in a rather more schematic fashion than we have met hitherto. The figures have the slight caricature air that also marks these scenes in the manuscripts just mentioned. Other pictures in this manuscript have architectural frames that show a profusion of *putti* blowing trumpets and gesticulating (see folio 7, the four Evangelists), while there are margins decorated with Renaissance candelabra decked with grotesque masks and

🔸 FIGURE 16 Calendar illustration for January.
Bodleian Library, Oxford, MS. Douce 72, folio 1 recto.

lustrous pearls – very similar to this is the decoration of MS.25 in Waddesdon
Manor, again a Rouen Use Book of Hours, dated by Delaissé to *c*.1510, which
has pictures for the labours of the months related (but not identical) to the set
we have been discussing.

There are similar borders in another Book of Hours of Rouen Use, now
MS.13 in the Society of Antiquaries in London. This is in a manner that has
absorbed some aspects of Renaissance style; the figures in the illustrations take
up a greater part of the area of the miniature and are often shown with
monumental, dramatic gestures. At some time in the sixteenth century, this
book was owned by Jean Dufour and Marguerite Austin or Autin; while this
provides ambiguous evidence for dating, it does link the manuscript with
people known to have belonged to Rouen families.[47] Stylistically, the manuscript belongs to the 1520s or 1530s. The calendar scenes (figure 17) are

⚜ FIGURE 17 Calendar illustrations for January and February.
Society of Antiquaries, London, MS.13, folios 1 recto and 2 recto.

identical in every respect to those in the Playfair Hours, even with the same *mise en page*, except as regards style. There can be no question but that the illuminator was using the same models as those used for these scenes in the Playfair Hours perhaps as much as forty years earlier in a totally different stylistic context. This is a phenomenon which we will come across again with other pictures in the Playfair Hours.

It is worth stressing the extreme similarity of the calendar pictures just mentioned. Distinguishing marks of the set are that the man feasting in the January scene is shown at a table set diagonally across the miniature; in the second scene, for February, the seated figure holds out both hands and a leg to the fire but speaks over his shoulder to a servant, who may or may not actually be shown by the miniaturist. This set is to be distinguished from variants current in Rouen in the last years of the fifteenth century. Here, the figure shown feasting for January is in a frontal position, with or without a figure on either side, and the table is set horizontally across the front of the miniature; the figure warming himself by the fire for February does not look over his shoulder or stretch a leg out to the fire, as he does in the Playfair series, but gazes into the flames with two hands outstretched and both feet on the ground. These versions are to be found in a number of Books of Hours of Rouen Use of the 1490s (Victoria and Albert Museum, Reid MS.11; Paris, Bibliothèque Nationale, ms. latin 1177) and in two related manuscripts of the early sixteenth century which include full-page miniatures in a Bourdichon-esque style, with fully rounded figures that take up a large area of the miniature and simple classical architectural settings with architectural frames that include gothic features such as niches for figures of saints and pointed arches with crockets (Edinburgh University Library, MS.304; Vienna, Österreichischen National-bibliothek, Cod.1954).[48] Another Rouen Book of Hours of *c.*1500 with a variant set of calendar illustrations is now in the Bodleian Library (Buchanan e 3): miniatures are framed by pillars festooned with pearls and borders where, among multicoloured acanthus, large carnations and other flowers are painted in a realistic fashion on grounds of liquid gold. The calendar illustration in another Rouen Book of Hours mentioned above, Waddesdon MS.25, dated to *c.*1510, follows these calendar scenes fairly closely but with some elements that echo the Playfair Hours pictures. It is as if a set of drawings was gradually evolving as successive copies of it were made. The Buchanan manuscript too has striking features which parallel the Playfair set; for instance, the man feasting in the January scene sits at a table positioned horizontally across the miniature but holds his right elbow high in the air as he drinks, just as he does in the Playfair Hours version. It may be the result of chance survival that these variant scenes appear in manuscripts that tend to be slightly later than the Playfair Hours itself. It remains to be discovered whether the use of these sets of illustrations can be found in earlier manuscripts dating back to the 1460s or 1450s.

Both these series of calendar illustrations are usually found executed in a lively, bold, and even crude manner. The ultimate source of the compositions appears to have been illustrations current in Paris in the early years of the fifteenth century. While it may not be possible to trace a direct and continuous pedigree leading back to the capital, the calendar illustrations of a Paris Book of Hours of 1410–1420, typical of its kind, show a more refined version of what appear to be the same compositions as the Playfair set, just as a similar Book of Hours with calendar illustrations attributed by Meiss to the Rohan workshop reveal the same pictorial ideas as the other Rouen sets.[49] One channel in which the variants mentioned above could have been introduced into the mainstream of Rouen illumination may be the Fastolf Master, who is thought to have worked in both Paris and the Norman capital: the calendar illustrations of the Sobieski Hours in which his work is found have striking resemblances with the Rouen sets, and this manuscript is held to have been begun in Paris and completed in Rouen in the third and fourth decades of the fifteenth century.[50] Reference to designs that were current in Paris earlier in that century does no more than underline the dominant position of that city where illumination was concerned, providing a pervasive and unifying influence for much illumination of a later date in France. What we have in Rouen illumination are sets of calendar pictures brought together to decorate 'middle-range-of-the market' manuscripts designed for swift execution and pleasing appearance, adapted from pictures whose history has a Paris connection. One only has to compare Jean Colombe's addition of the calendar illustration for November to the *Très Riches Heures* of the Duc de Berry in 1485 with the same picture in the Rouen sets to see how different interpretations could be made of a similar composition that had descended by totally different paths from a similar prototype.[51]

9. *Illumination: The Text*

D ELAISSÉ, a major authority on the history of Books of Hours, remarked in 1976 that manuscripts of this kind from Rouen in the late fifteenth century presented 'a near perfect homogeneity'.[52] Anyone looking at Books of Hours of Rouen Use which can be attributed to that city will be struck by the fact that limited numbers of compositions appear repeatedly in different combinations. Sometimes the compositions are executed in a manner that can be called no more than competent, at other times the manner is impressive. We appear to have a community of illuminators following a series of similar patterns. Like many of those who sit outside picture galleries in European capitals today, or in 'artistic' sites such as Montmartre in Paris, offering to sketch visitors for a small sum of money, the illuminators of some of the humbler workshops may have been unable to produce anything but the image they had produced for most of their career, so that portrayal of a particular subject gave the same result whoever wielded the brush. Not only whole compositions but also elements of compositions, re-assembled in different combinations, were used by the various workshops in late fifteenth century Rouen to provide Books of Hours with the requisite cycle of illustrations. What follows sets out to identify the different hands at work in the illumination of the Playfair Hours and to refer to a number of related manuscripts (a small sample, and one which could be vastly extended by systematic search) which throw some light on the way such books were produced.

There are seven distinct styles of painting to be found in the miniatures that illustrate the text of the Playfair Hours, so that it is likely that we are dealing with seven different miniaturists. The illumination of the calendar and text have been discussed separately, but it is an obvious question, and one that is not easy to answer, to ask whether the hand that decorated the calendar is also to be found with the text. Nowhere in the text can the walled backgrounds of the calendar miniatures be found, with the square blind windows with pink and green infill to represent rough stones. On the other hand, the 'matchstick' quality of the figures resemble in a general way the small scenes in the illustrations of the Hours of the Virgin Mary (plates XIII–XX). The calendar is likely to have been the last item added to the book before it was bound; the text is impersonal, and hence might be made with no specific client in view, whereas the calendar contains saints with a local attachment; the text is Sarum, for the British Isles, and the calendar narrows this down to Scotland to suit a Scottish customer. That the calendar miniaturist did indeed have a hand in the complete book is indicated by a single miniature, that of St Francis (plate XXVIb). This is extremely close as regards the depiction of the face and the convention used for trees (drops of dark green and a lighter green, not found elsewhere). If we take the calendar miniaturist to be a separate craftsman, perhaps a junior colleague of the major miniaturist in the manuscript, it may be that he was involved in the later stages of production, providing 'finishing touches', and inserting miniatures in folios overlooked by other illuminators, before the marginal decoration was put in. This last feature is constant throughout the manuscript, and uses the device common in fifteenth century French manuscripts of exploiting the transparency of the parchment to copy the design on the recto to trace a mirror image behind it on the verso of each folio.

The illustrators of the text are best considered in the ascending order of the extent of their contribution.

The first to be considered is that responsible for the small miniature of St Apollonia which shows two men extracting her teeth (plate XXXI). The saint's tormentors have costumes that are quite distinct from those found in the rest of the manuscript. The cap of the left-hand figure is not found elsewhere, nor are the proportions and animated poses of these dancing figures. The background is made up of luminous green, grey and blue washes; the figures throw small shadows on the ground. The colours, figures and the conventions for depicting trees identify this as the miniaturist responsible for the half-page miniatures of St Sebastian, St Erasmus and a number of others in EUL 43 (figure 18), as well as for a number of miniatures in the Farmor Hours (these two manuscripts are quite closely related: the composition for the illustration of the Office of the Dead, for example, is identical in each).

Another hand which played a similarly small part in decorating the Playfair Hours is that responsible for the scene of the Assumption (plate XI). Alone of the miniatures in the manuscript, this takes up the whole of the top half of the page; the simple architectural frame brings the miniature to the fullest width of the page. The decision to do this was evidently that of the miniaturist; the decoration that fills the bottom half of the page was left for the illuminator that

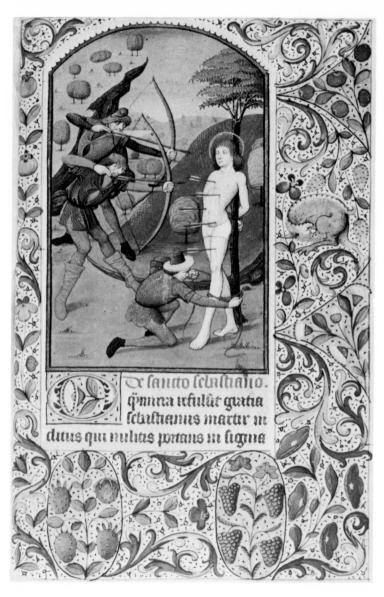

De sancto sebastiano.
Q[uem] mira refulsit gr[ati]a
sebastia[n]us martir in
clitus qui nullas portans in signia

✤ FIGURE 18 The Martyrdom of St Sebastian.
Edinburgh University Library, MS.43, folio 147 recto.

went through the book once all gatherings had been assembled and put in the marginal decoration. The aerial effects of this full-page miniature, with the central figure full-length and suspended against the sky, are matched in the picture of the Transfiguration of Christ in a Rouen Book of Hours of slightly later date than the Playfair manuscript, now in Edinburgh, EUL 306 (figure 19). The haloes here are indicated by a circle of brushed gold, rather than by a solid disc of gold as in the Playfair Hours. This feature of the Playfair Hours is also found in a picture from a Rouen Book of Hours now in Cherbourg (Bibliothèque Municipale, MS.5) that follows the same model as that of the

⚜ FIGURE 19 The Transfiguration of Christ.
Edinburgh University Library, MS.306, folio 22 verso.

Transfiguration in the Edinburgh manuscript just mentioned; Lafond dates this manuscript to the early sixteenth century and ascribes it to miniaturists working for Georges d'Amboise – certainly most of the illustrations in this manuscript seem to be quite different from those usually found in Rouen Books of Hours and form an original cycle of pictures for a book of this kind.[53] Of the same date is another Rouen Book of Hours, N LS 6129, very much the product of 'indigenous' Rouen illumination, with a Pentecost scene (folio 92 verso) that may even be by the same hand as the Playfair Hours picture of the Assumption, or at least following a related model (figure 20). The manner of this miniaturist is characterised by faces with bulbous noses, large areas filled with a simple monochrome wash, and the use of bright orange for clothes and for angels.

Three miniatures appearing on the twenty-second gathering of the Playfair Hours (folios 168–171) appear to be the work of another illuminator (plates XXVIc, XXVII, XXVIII). They are characterised by the delicacy of the painting – which is the best in the manuscript – and by the rich blue pigment used for the backgrounds. The miniatures consist of a seven-line picture of St Veronica showing the veil with the Holy Face, a full-page miniature of two angels holding a chalice containing the wound of Christ against a background of three large nails, and a crucifix scene with the full range of implements associated with the Passion – the cock in this last scene is a particularly delicate example of the neatness of this hand.

Another very distinctive hand, and one which made a significant contribution to our manuscript, is that responsible for the picture of St Jerome and a number of others (plates XXIII, XXIVa, XXV, XXVId, XXIX, XXX, XXXII). The brushwork is immediately distinguished by its painterly quality and the muddiness of the palette. Parts of the figures and other features in these paintings are bordered by a black outline, very striking when left revealed, as with the right leg of the murderer of St Thomas a Becket. The faces too are distinctive, modelled, rather clumsily, with grey, pink and white; eye-lids are emphasised with grey modelling. The halo is consistently of a solid disc of brushed gold within a clearly visible black line; a little way within the outer circumference is another black line. Most of this painter's work is on separate gatherings: the burial scene is the only decoration on the 16th (folios 120–7), the picture of Christ lamented by the Virgin and Apostles the only miniature on the 18th (folios 136–143), the portrait of St Jerome the only picture on the 20th (folios 152–9). However, his work is also found on two *bifolia* of the 23rd

Dñiñc labia mca

apcrics

Et os mcū au

🌼 FIGURE 20 Pentecost scene.
National Library of Scotland, MS.6129, folio 92 recto.

gathering – miniatures of St Christopher (a composition similar to that in E U L 43, folio 142), St George and the Martyrdom of St Thomas a Becket on folios 173 verso, 174 verso and 176 – where another hand's work is to be found on the other *bifolia*.

This other hand was that which painted most of the small nine-line or seven-line miniatures illustrating the suffrages to the saints (plates XXIVb & c, XXVIa). His or her manner is characterised by simple washes of colour over ruled lines that recede towards a central point to indicate floor tiles, backgrounds made up of red or blue brocade, and walls of grey pierced with windows that have slightly rounded tops and diamond-shaped wire infills (these were painted in silver that has now tarnished). Haloes are solid discs of brushed gold with a clear black outline. Most distinctive are the faces, small neat lines for eyes, bottom of the nose and mouth (eye-brows are in light grey), and a dot of cherry-red for the lips, sometimes too for the cheeks. It might be argued that this manner was one adopted by some of the other artists at work on the Playfair Hours when tackling this series of small miniature scenes, were it not for the fact that this illuminator was also responsible for a large half-page miniature, that of the Virgin and Child enthroned (plate X). Treatment of this scene evidences the same mannerisms as the small miniatures just mentioned. The simplicity of composition to be found in these also characterises the larger scale work; the throne itself is of a more frugal kind than the many others to be seen in other pictures in the Playfair Hours.

The chief artist at work in the Playfair Hours was responsible for a number of miniatures all of which consist of a major subject and subsidiary scenes. The miniatures in question are those of the four Evangelists on folio 13 (plate IX), the Pietà on folio 31 verso (plate XII), David in Penitence on folio 80 (plate XXI), the figures of death attacking horsemen on folio 100 (plate XXII), and the set of illustrations for the Hours of the Virgin themselves (plates XIII–XX). These miniatures are of two sorts. The first comprises a half-page miniature with a subsidiary scene in the decoration of the outer and bottom borders. The border decoration here is like that of the rest of the book except that it surrounds all four sides of the page and is liable to have compartments of contrasting red and blue grounds upon which are floral motifs in brushed gold. Since borders of this kind are also to be found with miniatures executed by other hands, we can take it that this decoration was the work of a single craftsman, perhaps working with an assistant, responsible for the whole book.

The second sort of miniature covers the whole page, so that there is no need for any border decoration. We have a regular division of the page, with a major subject flanked by two scenes in the outer margin and two in the lower register. For the picture of death attacking horsemen, there is no frame other than a floral design on a ribbon of brushed gold. For all the other full-page miniatures, architectural frames are used. Most elaborate is that of the first illustration to the Hours of the Virgin: two pillars, in blue with fleurs-de-lys painted on them, support capitals and decorated, flattened arches with central point painted in brushed gold; on the capitals are figures of Adam and Eve eating the forbidden fruit. This display fitted the beginning of the most crucial part of the book; the frames for the full page miniatures of the Nativity and David in Penitence are much more simple.

The manner of this miniaturist can be characterised by a number of features: use of a bright yellow-green for distant fields in landscapes (especially on upland rocky crags), a 'match-stick' quality given to figures in the smallest scenes, women shown with turban head-dresses looking as if they were made up of white bandages drawn with a red outline, an emphasis upon heavily-drawn eyebrows to give expressions to the human face. In contrast to the other miniaturists, the colours are not painted sufficiently densely to prevent the ruled lines of the page from being visible.

It was said above that Rouen Books of Hours were characterised by their homogenous quality and by the variety of hands that can be seen contributing to their decoration. Parallels to compositions in the Playfair Hours are not difficult to find. Closely similar compositions, with similarities most marked in the depiction of human figures, are carried out in a manner that varies and at different levels of competence. It is not proposed to give an exhaustive list of comparisons for the compositions found in the Playfair Hours, but rather to indicate in what kind of manuscript they are to be found and over what sort of chronological span they were used. It should be said at the outset that the dating of Books of Hours of this kind, produced 'en série' and at a level of finish to satisfy the 'middle range' of the market, is particularly difficult. However, if we place the Playfair Hours at some point in the 1480s or early 1490s, we are able to distribute related manuscripts in a coherent pattern around it.

Of a slightly earlier date than our manuscript is a Rouen Use Book of Hours now in the Bodleian Library, Douce 253. It is a much more finished product than the Playfair Hours; Pächt and Alexander date it to c.1480 and relate it to

FIGURE 21 The Four Evangelists.
Bodleian Library, Oxford, MS. Douce 253, folio 13 recto.

the group of manuscripts now known as that of the Master of the Geneva
Latini. The large initials in this manuscript have a trefoil decoration and gilded
grounds, belonging to an earlier tradition. Much of the border decoration is like
that of the Playfair Hours, though there are also borders with a shining
brushed gold ground on which are sprays of flowers and white acanthus leaves
with grey undersides, grotesques and realistically painted birds. This Douce
manuscript is closely related to a Rouen Book of Hours at Waddesdon Manor,
MS.12, which Delaissé dates to *c*.1470. In both manuscripts, the Annunciation
scene is accompanied by the decorative device in the lower margin of a
fountain, the source of a stream in which birds play.

✤ FIGURE 22 The Four Evangelists.
National Library of Scotland, MS.6129, folio 13 recto.

The scenes of the Evangelists in Douce 253 (figure 21), which has the typically Rouen feature of portraying the figures in a half-page miniature divided by a frame into four quarters, are all similar to those in the Playfair Hours, though St Luke's ox has changed into a lion, designating him as St Mark.

A number of other scenes in Douce 253 are similar to those in the Playfair Hours. The Annunciation has an identical canopy over the Virgin, and the positioning of the figures is little different. Even closer to the Annunciation in Douce 253 is that in EUL 43 (figure 23). Based on the same model as these scenes is the Annunciation in a Rouen Use Book of Hours now in New York

(Pierpont Morgan Library, M 220), dated to the 1490s by John Plummer.[54]
The pillars that frame the miniature are surmounted by figures of Adam and
Eve almost identical to those in the Playfair Annunciation. This link between
the two manuscripts is confirmed by the subsidiary scenes in the New York
miniature showing the Meeting at the Golden Gate and the Presentation of
Mary at the Temple, composed in precisely the same fashion as these scenes in
the Playfair Hours.

Another Rouen Use Book of Hours mentioned earlier as having the same set
of calendar illustrations as the Playfair Hours, is EUL 306. Slightly later in date

Edinburgh University Library, MS.306, folio 23 recto.

than our manuscript, it has the same Evangelists' portraits but with St John occupying most of the miniature and the others in three compartments underneath the three lines of text. The picture of the Annunciation differs little from that in the Playfair Hours (figure 24): the angel wears a chasuble rather than a cloak; the architectural arch over Virgin and angel is not faceted and the figures of Adam and Eve that surmount it are shown being tempted by a serpent; angel and Virgin are dressed in gold brocade rather than in blue, countryside is visible through a door behind the angel. Three of the subsidiary scenes in EUL 306 are also very close (Golden Gate, Presentation, Marriage of Mary and

Joseph). The Nativity scene in this manuscript follows the same composition as that in the Playfair Hours, the position of the animals' heads (in profile, ass looking back over its head in the opposite direction from the ox) being a characteristic feature.[55] The picture of Moses removing his shoes in front of the burning bush is identical in each manuscript. Compositions found in EUL 306 also crop up in some of the manuscripts mentioned earlier. The picture of the figures of death attacking horsemen is identical to that in Pierpont Morgan Library M 220, Victoria and Albert Museum, Reid MS.11, and CUL Add.4099, as well as to that in the Yester Hours, and the scene of David in Penitence matches that in the New York manuscript. Correspondences of this kind could be traced pretty well *ad infinitum* in Rouen Books of Hours of this date. If EUL 306 is to be dated later than the Playfair Hours, the reason must lie in part in its border decoration, which consists of the same kind of foliage but depicted in a much simpler way; like NLS 6129, it has a more 'sketchy' appearance generally than the Playfair Hours.

The same can be said both as regards date and manner of execution of another Rouen Use Book of Hours, CUL Add.4099 (figures 5, 7, 11, 25). This too used the same set of calendar pictures as the Playfair Hours, though in an abbreviated form. The Annunciation scene (figure 25) with its three subsidiary miniatures provides some close comparisons with the Playfair Hours' treatment of the same subject, as does the Nativity scene and a number of others. Flowers in the margins here are becoming much more realistically drawn, and poppies and pansies can just be recognised.

Thus far there is very little to show that the manuscripts mentioned were in fact produced over a period of time, since dating by style scarcely allows great precision with manuscripts of this quality. However, differences between them do show that people working in a rather different manner and levels of competence were using the same compositions. A Rouen Book of Hours in Cambridge, Fitzwilliam 76, is another that can be adduced to show this: the figures in the portraits of the four Evangelists on folio 13 or in the elaborate Annunciation scene on folio 27 (three of the marginal scenes here are very close to those in the Playfair Hours) are executed in a much finer fashion than in all

⚜ FIGURE 25 The Annunciation.
Cambridge University Library, Add.MS.4099, folio 29 recto.

Dunne labia mea
apxies. Ct os meum an
nunciabit laudem tuam.

✤ FIGURE 26 The Annunciation.
National Library of Scotland, MS.6129, folio 25 recto.

auuplo Placebo domino. ps.
Ilra qm oraudict
dominus voern
oroms mee.

⚜ FIGURE 27 Burial scene.
Bodleian Library, Oxford, MS. Douce 253, folio 100 recto.

✣ FIGURE 28 Burial scene.
Bodleian Library, Oxford, MS. Buchanan e 13, folio 97 recto.

🌺 FIGURE 29 Burial scene.
Bodleian Library, Oxford, MS. Rawl. liturg. f 24, folio 77 recto.

manuscripts mentioned apart from Douce 253. M.R. James dated this manuscript to the 1490s. Use of these compositions survived a fundamental change in style and can be found after the Renaissance manner had been established as the norm. In Buchanan e 3, we find not only calendar pictures similar to those in the Playfair Hours but also an Annunciation with subsidiary scenes, a Nativity scene with an accompanying picture of Moses (figure 9), an Adoration of the Magi, Presentation at the Temple and Coronation of the Virgin, which follow the compositions of the Playfair Hours very closely and on occasion appear identical. The architectural frames on some of these miniatures, with their hanging chains of pearls, oblige us to date it after 1500; the convention for the depiction of walls with blind square windows of green and pink and classical fluted columns (very schematically drawn) seen here can be found in a happily dated piece of illumination, the *Livre de fondation de la communauté des chirurgiens de Rouen* of 1518; while this is a feature, like the architectural canopy shown in the book, that occurs in earlier manuscripts, it supports a sixteenth century date for the Buchanan manuscript.[56] The same can be said for another Bodleian manuscript, Douce 72, which uses the same calendar illustrations as the Playfair Hours. The marginal decoration of this manuscript relates it to MS.25 at Waddesdon Manor, another Rouen Use Book of Hours which Delaissé dates to *c.*1510.[57] A further Book of Hours of this kind which follows the same compositions as the Playfair Hours miniatures but which must be dated after 1500 is NLS 6129, mentioned above as using the same calendar illustrations as our manuscript. Most impressive of all as an example of a composition surviving a change in style is Fitzwilliam 106, a Rouen Use Book of Hours. The scene of the three horsemen being attacked by three figures of death here is identical to that in the Playfair Hours, except that the architectural details are quite un-medieval (figure 30). This phenomenon is comparable to the use in Antiquaries 13 of the same pictures as were used for the calendar illustrations in the Playfair Hours at an earlier date. Like Fitzwilliam 106, Antiquaries 13 can be dated to *c.*1520; the Annunciation to the Shepherds scene on folio 51 follows the same composition as that in EUL 43, (figures 2 and 3), which is again of the same date as the Playfair Hours, that is to say the 1480s.

FIGURE 30 Three horsemen attacked by three figures of death. Fitzwilliam Museum, Cambridge, MS.106, folio 56 verso.

Continuity in the use of these compositions seems to allow us to identify the traditions of 'indigenous' book production in Rouen, as opposed to the work of artists such as the Master of Petrarch's Triumphs who are thought to have brought a different kind of illumination to Rouen at the time that Georges d'Amboise was archbishop (1499–1510) and whose work was certainly distinguished from that of indigenous production in that much of it was for members of the French royal court.

It was mentioned above that an illuminator known as the Master of the Geneva Latini was active in Rouen at the beginning of the second half of the fifteenth century.[58] Much work needs to be done before the *œuvre* of this Master can be put together and hence the degree of his influence on Rouen illumination in the second half of the fifteenth century established. The work that has been ascribed to this artist is certainly of very good quality.

If the attribution to him made by John Plummer of a Rouen Use Book of Hours in New York (Private Collection) is accepted,[59] then he certainly had some link with some of the manuscripts mentioned in connection with the Playfair Hours: the scene of the Annunciation to the Shepherds is close to that in EUL 43 which is itself extremely close to this illustration in the Farmor Hours, though the hand may not be the same. One feature in the manuscript singled out by Plummer is the depiction of what looks like a fir tree in the landscape distances behind the figures. This convention, distinctive enough, is only found in one of the manuscripts we have been considering, and one distinguished by the quality of its painting: Douce 253, attributed by Pächt and Alexander to the Geneva Latini group. It is worth remarking that the same convention appears in two other manuscripts associated with this Master, both of them Rouen Use Book of Hours (Paris, Bibliothèque de l'Arsenal, MS.562; H.P. Kraus, Catalogue 117, no.12)[60] though details in scenes such as the Visitation do not match those found in the Playfair Hours and other manuscripts mentioned above.

The magnificent Book of Hours of Coutances Use, plausibly dated to *c.*1460–1475, that was sold at Sotheby's on 6 December 1983 (lot 82), has also been attributed to this Master.[61] A number of compositions in this manuscript are to be found in some of the books we have been considering. The Betrayal of Christ by Judas, the Transfiguration and the architectural frame for the Annunciation, for example, are identical to those, admittedly of inferior execution, in NLS 6131, which is of the 1490s. There are certain stylistic similarities between the miniaturist of the Hours' illustrations in the Playfair Hours and pictures in the Sotheby's manuscript; particularly striking are the upland plateaux on rocky crags and the depiction of distant buildings. The marginal picture of the Baptism of Christ and the Pietà in the Playfair Hours (plates XIV, XII) are identical to these scenes in the Sotheby's manuscript, and the Assumption of the Virgin (plate XI) is also very close, but the quality of the painting is not as good and can hardly be seen as issuing from the same, or a successor, workshop. However, two hands found in the Playfair Hours, that responsible for the St Apollonia miniature (plate XXXI) and that responsible for the St Veronica, Wound of Christ and Instruments of the Passion miniatures (plates XXVIc, XXVII, XXVIII) are of a distinctive quality and style which can be paralleled in the Sotheby's manuscript, so that we can perhaps think of their having been trained in the immediate circle of the Master of the Geneva Latini. A number of scenes in EUL 43 by the St Apollonia miniaturist (The martyrdom of St Sebastian, the Visitation, the Annunciation to the Shepherds and the Pietà in particular) show both compositions and stylistic details very similar to the corresponding scenes in the Sotheby's manuscript, while others, such as the martyrdom of St Thomas a Becket, are likewise based on the same compositions in the Sotheby's manuscript.

These correspondences may indicate that some of the hands evidenced in our manuscript can be regarded as 'followers' of the Geneva Latini Master in so far as the compositions followed were related. No doubt future research will clarify this point. Rouen Books of Hours of the second half of the fifteenth century of the kind typified by the Playfair Hours have a distinct character when compared with those produced in the city earlier in the century, where affinities are close to those Parisian manuscripts associated with the names of the Boucicaut and Bedford Hours Masters.[62] Indeed, Porcher in 1960 went so far as to suggest that the Bedford Master's workshop moved to Rouen, though many authorities today are less inclined to explain the diffusion of models by the actual movements of whole workshops.[63] John Plummer has suggested that the major influence on Rouen illumination after c.1450 was a Paris miniaturist such as the Jean Rollin II Master,[64] and it may well be to a source such as this that we should look for the origins of the compositions that were reproduced by so many hands to achieve the 'near perfect homogeneity' which, according to Delaissé, characterised manuscript book production in Rouen at the time that the Playfair Hours was produced.

10. *Conclusion*

THIS discussion of the Playfair Hours has revealed a number of points about its history, as well as drawing attention to the commercial environment in which it was produced. The manuscript dates from the 1480s or thereabouts, and represents the work of a number of craftsmen, including seven miniaturists, whose efforts are likely to have been co-ordinated by a bookseller or *libraire* on behalf of a particular customer. The Use of the Hours of the Virgin and the Office of the Dead is that of Sarum, showing that it was intended for use by someone in or from the British Isles. The calendar appended to the book before it was finally bound up indicates that the intended owner was Scottish. The calendar illustrations come from a set used by a number of Rouen illuminators in the late fifteenth century and which was still in use by miniaturists working in a different style in the 1520s–1530s. The other illustrations are based on compositions commonly followed by the illuminators of Books of Hours in late fifteenth century Rouen, compositions which also continued to be used in the early sixteenth century. The Playfair Hours represents the kind of book produced in large numbers in Rouen in the last quarter of the fifteenth century, decorated with a distinctive repertory of compositions that serve to distinguish this group from Rouen illumination of the first half of the century. The numbers in which they survive show that the advent of printed books did not entail the immediate collapse of traditional methods of book production. The uniform quality noticed in the manuscripts compared with the Playfair Hours may indeed represent a 'stream-lining' of methods of production, adopted to cope with increased demand or even to compete with the products of the printing press, a speculation that seems to be supported by the apparent abundance in which these late fifteenth century Rouen Use Book of Hours survive today.

11. *Description of the Manuscript*

BOOK OF HOURS (USE OF SARUM)
France (Rouen), s.xv ex. (1480s)

1. folios 1–12v. Calendar, entries alternately in blue and red, with major feasts in gold.
2. folios 13–17v. Gospel pericopes: John I, 1–15; Luke I, 26–38; Matthew II, 1–12; Mark XVI, 14–20; ends with prayer to the Virgin Mary beginning: Ave domina sancta Maria, mater dei, regina celi.
3. folios 18–35v. Prayers to the Virgin Mary.
   (i) *Oratio saluberrima ac devotissima de beata Maria virgine dei genitrice.*
   Obsecro te . . . ego sum facturus . . . et michi famulo tuo . . .
   (ii) prayer of 13 verses, each beginning 'Ave Maria', and the first: Ave Maria ancilla Trinitatis.
   (iii) *Septem gaudia spiritulia* [sic] *beate Marie virginis composita per beatum Thomam Cantuar'.*
   (iv) Five joys of the Virgin Mary beginning: Gaude virgo mater Christi.
   (v) O illustrissima et excellentissima.
   (vi) *Septem gaudia beate Marie dei genitricis que habuit in terris*: [lacks 1st folio; begins abruptly:] pariendo non gravaris.
   (vii) Memento obsecro dulcis mater.
   (viii) *Oratio devotissima de beata Maria*: O Intemerata.
   (ix) Stabat mater dolorosa.
4. folios 36–79v. Hours of the Virgin Mary, Use of Sarum, with Hours of the Cross worked in. Suffrages after Lauds are as follows:

   (i) Holy Spirit
   (ii) Trinity
   (iii) Holy Cross
   (iv) Michael
   (v) John the Baptist
   (vi) Peter and Paul
   (vii) Andrew
   (viii) Stephen
   (ix) Lawrence
   (x) George
   (xi) Thomas
   (xii) Sebastian
   (xiii) Nicholas
   (xiv) Anthony
   (xv) Anna
   (xvi) Mary Madeleine
   (xvii) Katherine
   (xviii) Margaret
   (xix) Barbara
   (xx) All Saints
   (xxi) Peace
   (xxii) Cross

77

5. folios 80–99v. Penitential Psalms, Gradual Psalms and Litany.
6. folios 100–124v. Office of the Dead (Use of Sarum).
7. folios 125–138v. Commendationes animarum.
8. folios 139–144. Psalms of the Passion.
9. folios 144v–148v. Prayers and Suffrages of the Sacrament.

    (i) *De sancto sacramento altaris. Antiphona*: Angelorum esca nutrivisti populum tuum.

    (ii) *Orationes devotissime dicende in elevatione corporis Christi*: Ave vere corpus.

    (iii) Anima Christi sanctifica me.

    (iv) *Salutacio ad sanguinem Ihesu Christi*: Ave vere sanguis.

    (v) Salve sancta caro.

    (vi) Domine Ihesu Christe qui hanc sacratissimam carnem.

    (vii) Domine Ihesu Christe, rex gloriosissime, cuius magnitudinem.

    (viii) Domine Ihesu Christe qui ex voluntate patris.

    (ix) Domine non secundum peccata nostra.

    (x) Precor te piissime domine.

10. folios 148v–151v. Prayers to the Father, Son, Holy Ghost and Trinity.

    (i) *Oratio ad Deum patrem omnipotentem*: Domine sancte pater omnipotens eterne Deus qui coequalem.

    (ii) *Oratio ad Ihesum Christum*: Fili redemptor mundi Deus.

    (iii) *Oratio ad sanctum spiritum*: Spiritus sancte Deus, miserere nobis. Domine spiritus sancte Deus qui coequalis.

    (iv) *Oratio ad sanctam trinitatem*: Domine deus omnipotens eterne et ineffabilis.

    (v) O bone Ihesu scribe in corde meo.

11. folios 152–165v. Psalter of St Jerome, ending with a prayer, *Oratio*: Omnipotens sempiterne deus, clementiam tuam.
12. folios 166–167. Verses of St Bernard.
13. folio 167. Suffrage to St Francis.
14. folios 168–171v. Prayers to the Holy Face, God the Father, and Christ.

    (i) Salve sancta facies.

    (ii) Deus qui nobis famulis tuis.

    (iii) Domine Ihesu Christe qui manus tuas.

    (iv) Benedictio dei patris cum angelis suis sit super me.

    (v) Domine Ihesu Christe fili Dei vivi.

15. folios 172–182v. Suffrages to the Saints. One folio missing, begins abruptly with St James.

(i) James

(ii) Christopher

(iii) George

(iv) Thomas a Becket of Canterbury

(v) Anne

(vi) Mary Magdalene

(vii) Katherine

(viii) Margaret

(ix) Barbara

(x) Apollonia

16. folios 183–192v. Twenty three prayers to Christ, the first beginning: O bone Ihesu, O dulcissime Ihesu, O piissime Ihesu, O Ihesu fili Marie . . ., the last: O domine Ihesu Christe pastor bone.

17. folios 193–194v. Prayers to God and the archangel Michael.

(i) *Oratio devota ad Deum*: Deus propitius esto mihi.

(ii) *De sancto Michiale* [sic]: Sancte Michael archangele domini nostri Ihesu Christi qui venisti.

18. folios 194–195v. *Oratio saluberrima atque devota de septem verbis Ihesu Christi in cruce pendentis*. Ends abruptly, last folio missing.

19. folios 196–203v. Gospels according to St John, chapters 18 and 19. One folio missing, begins abruptly: suis trans torrentem Cedron ubi erat ortus.

ff. iv + 203 + iii. 175 × 115 mm. Written space: 95 × 60 mm. (calendar: 95 × 64 mm.). 19 lines (calendar: 22 lines). Ruling in red ink. Collation: 1^{12}, 2^8, 3^8 wants 1 before fol.27, $4–9^8$, 10^4, $11–21^8$, 22^4, 23^8 wants 1 before fol.172, 24^4, 25^8 wants 1 before fol.184, 26^6, singleton missing, 27^8. Written in *lettre bâtarde*. Calendar with illustrations for labours of the month and zodiac signs. Full-page pictures for Matins and Prime of Hours of the Virgin, Penitential Psalms, Office of the Dead and Plea for Benediction (fol.169v). Half-page miniatures with two subsidiary scenes for art.2, 3(viii), Hours of the Virgin other than Matins and Prime. Half-page miniatures for arts.3(i), 3(iii), 7 (beginning and end), 11, 14(v), 15(iii), 15(iv). Seven-line to ten-line miniatures for arts. 3(v), 9(i), 10(i), 10(ii), 10(iii), 10(iv), 13, 14(i), 15(i), 15(ii), 15(v) to 15(ix), 19 (on fol.202). Eleven line miniature across whole written space for art.15(x). Initials: 2-, 3- and 4-line are of white foliate shapes with grey shading on red letter-shape, the whole on grounds of brushed gold with naturalistic sprays of flowers or fruit. 1-line initials are of brushed gold on monochrome russet-red or blue grounds with brushed gold foliate highlighting; line-fillers to match. Binding of early nineteenth century, English or Scottish, retaining boards of mid-sixteenth century French binding. Secundo folio (fol.14) *eum non receperunt*.

Written in France (Rouen). Arms, sixteenth century(?): Barry of 6, argent & sable; Argent, 3 bars gules. Owned by 'Dame Charlotte' in 1564. Inscribed in an eighteenth century French hand: 'Lemiere 8 [*or* s] . i. d'. In nineteenth century, owned by ancestors of the Rev Dr Patrick M. Playfair of St Andrews, who sold it in June 1918 on behalf of the Scottish Red Cross; bought by Sir Otto Beit and presented to the V&A Museum.

12. *Colour Plates*

NOTE

All illustrations in the Playfair Hours are reproduced in the colour plates, with the exception of the following small (7-line to 9-line) miniatures: folio 25, Virgin and Child in mandorla; folio 149, God enthroned; folio 149 verso, Ecce Homo; folio 177 verso, St Anne; folio 178 verso, Mary Magdalene; folio 179 verso, St Katherine; folio 180 verso, St Margaret. These are all by the miniaturist responsible for the pictures reproduced on plates X, XXIV(b) & (c), and XXVI(a).

Ianuarius habet dies xxxi.
Luna xxx.

iiii	A	Circunciſio domini.
	b	iiii Oct ſancti iohannis.
xi	c	iii Oct de ſancto iohanne
	d	ii Oct ſanctorum innocentium.
xix	e	Vigilia
viii	f	id Epyphania domini.
	g	id Sancti yſidori epiſcopi.
xvi		id Luciani martiris.
v	b	id Sancti feſam epi et cõfeſſ.
	c	id Pauli primi heremite.

Plate I   81

Februarius habet dies xxviij.
Luna xxix.

		d		Brigide virginis.
xi		e N̄	Purificatio beate marie.
xix		f N̄	Blasij epi et martinis.
viij		g N̄	
		N̄	Agathe virginis et mīie.
xvi	b	Id	Dorothee virginis.
v	c	Id	helene regine.
	d	Id	Appoloine virginie et mīie
xiij	e	Id	Sancti ausberti arch.

Martius habet dies xxxi.
Luna xxix.

m   d   Monam epi. Albini epi.
     e Al   Paule virgine et mris.
xi   f Al   Maturim epi.
     g Al   Adriani martiris
xix   Al   Eusebii martiris.
viii b Al   Saldredi epi.
     c Al   Perpetue et felicitatie virgȝ
xvi d Id   Cypriani epi et conf̄
v   e Id   Constantini regis et mris
     f Id   Lessoin epi et conf̄.

Plate III   83

Aprilis habet dies xxx.
Luna xxix.

	g		
xi	A	Nl	Marie egipciace.
	b	Nl	Richardi epi.
xix	c	Nl	Ambrosij epi.
vm	d	Nl	Maximiani epi.
xvi	e	Id	Sixti pape et mīs.
v	f	Id	Alexandri epi.
	g	Id	Auertini martiris.
xiii	A	Id	Hugonis archiepi.
ij	b	Id	

Mayus habet dies xxxi.
Luna xxx.

xi	b	Philippi et iacobi aplorum
	c KL	Athanasy epi et conff.
xix	d KL	Inuentio sancte crucis.
viii	e KL	festum corone dñi.
	f KL	Gotardi epi et conff.
xvi	g KL	Johis ante portam latina.
v	KL	Cleti pape et martiris.
	b Id	
xiii	c Id	translatio sci nicholay.
ii	d Id	Gordiani et epimachi mr.

Plate V   85

(a)

(b)

(c)

86   Plate VI

(a)

(b)

(c)

Plate VII   87

December habet dies xxxi.
Luna xxx

f   Eligii epi.
xiiii M Candidi martiris.
n M
x b M Barbare virgis et mris.
c M Sabbe abbatis.
xviii d Id Nicholay epi et conf.
vii e Id Oct sancti andree.
f Id Conceptio beate marie virg
xv g Id
iiii Id Valerie virg Eulalie virg

Beaundum iohannem.
N prinaipio erat verbu:
et verbum erat apud deu.

Plate IX   89

Aude flore virginali.
honorega stituali. trā
cendeus splendiseru.

Plate XI   91

Intemerata et meter
num benedicta singu
laris atqz incompara

DOMINE LABIA MEA APERIES ET OS MEVM

Plate XIII   93

us in adiutorium
meum intende.
ne ad adiuua
dum me festina.

Plate XV   95

Eus m adiutoriú
meum intende
omme ad adiu

Plate XVII   97

Eus in Adiutoriu
adiutoriu meu intede
ne ad adiuuandum

Plate XIX   99

Omnerte nos deus
salutaris noster.
Et auerte iram

Plate XXI 101

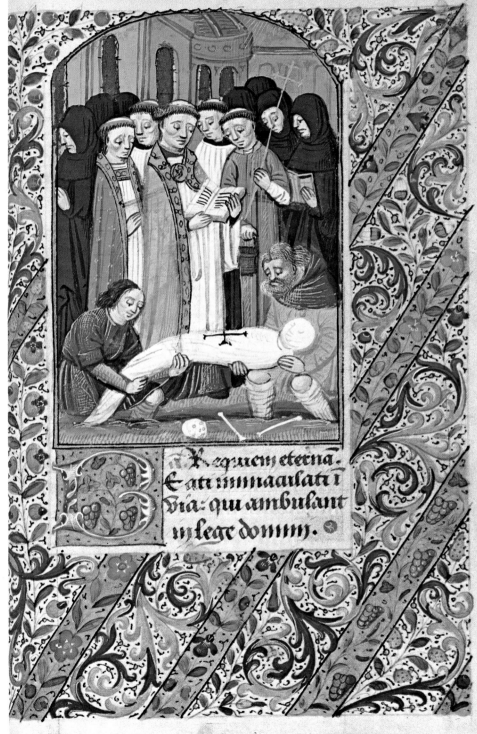

Requiem eternā.
Eati immaailati i
via: qui ambulant
ī lege domini.

Plate XXIII   103

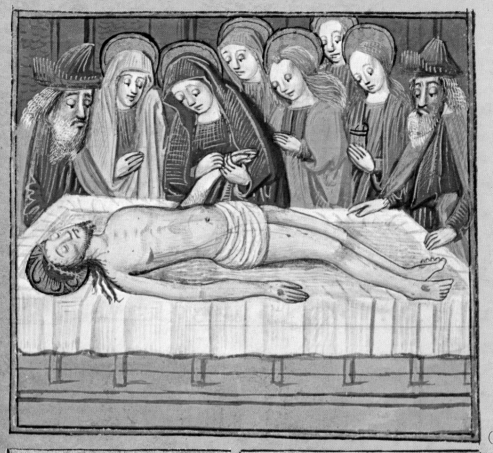

(a)

(b)

(c)

Erba mea auribue
percipe domine itelli
ge clamorem meu.
ntende voci orationis mee rex

Plate XXV   105

a)

(b)

(c)

(d)

Plate XXVII   107

De sancto georgio. an̄t.
Eorum martir inclite
te decet laus et gloria

Plate XXIX 109

melliflua caritate oium peccator
noftrozum multitudinem coo
perire digneris. Qui viuis
et regnas deus per omnia fecla
feculorum Amen.

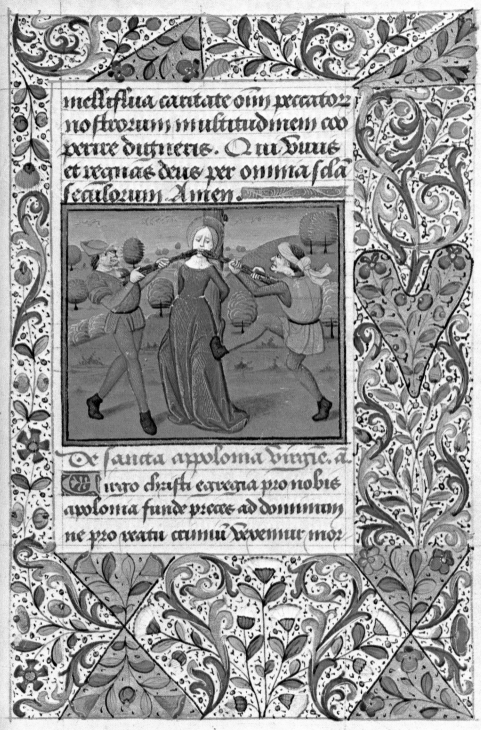

De fancta appolonia virgie. ã.
Ingto chrifti egregia pro nobis
appolonia funde preces ad dominum
ne pro reatu criminu veniamus mor

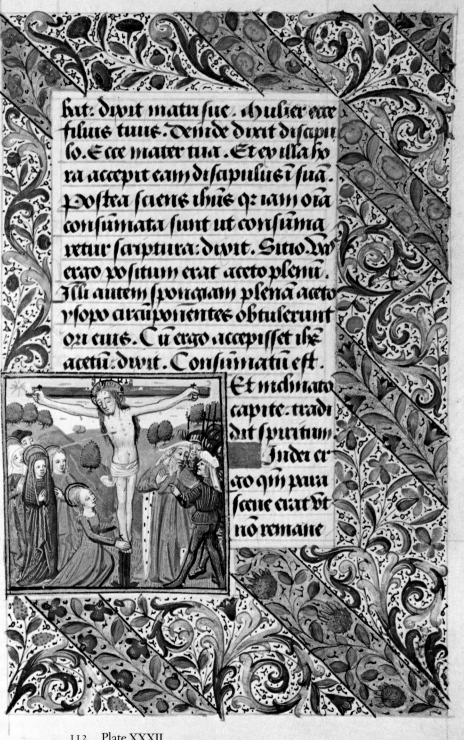

13. *Captions to Colour Plates*

Plate I.   *Folio 1 recto.* Calendar illustration for January: man feasting, waited upon by two servants.

Plate II.   *Folio 2 recto.* Calendar illustration for February: man warming himself at a fire, with servant bringing fuel.

Plate III.   *Folio 3 recto.* Calendar illustration for March: three men pruning.

Plate IV.   *Folio 4 recto.* Calendar illustration for April: man gathering flowers for a woman.

Plate V.   *Folio 5 recto.* Calendar illustration for May: man and woman on horseback hawking.

Plate VI.   (a) *Folio 6 recto.* Calendar illustration for June: man scything and a woman gathering hay with a rake.
              (b) *Folio 7 recto.* Calendar illustration for July: man reaping, with another binding sheaves of corn.
              (c) *Folio 8 recto.* Calendar illustration for August: two men threshing.

Plate VII.   (a) *Folio 9 recto.* Calendar illustration for September: man carrying grapes with another treading them.
              (b) *Folio 10 recto.* Calendar illustration for October: man sowing with a woman carrying a sack of seed.
              (c) *Folio 11 recto.* Calendar illustration for November: man knocking down acorns for pigs, and a woman with a distaff.

Plate VIII.   *Folio 12 recto.* Calendar illustration for December: man slaughtering pig, with a man and woman collecting pig's blood.

Plate IX.   *Folio 13 recto.* Gospel pericopes. The four Evangelists with their symbols: St John on the Isle of Patmos with an eagle holding the inkwell; St Mathew with an angel; St Mark with a lion; St Luke with an ox. The division of this miniature into four quarters is a characteristic mark of Rouen book illumination. *Outer margin:* St John the Baptist pointing to his symbol the Lamb of God, who is to relieve the world of its sins. *Lower margin:* John the Evangelist boiled in oil; according to legend, the Emperor Domitian ordered John to come to Rome where his head was shaved prior to his being boiled in oil at the *Porta Latina,* from which he emerged unscathed.

| Plate X. | *Folio 18 recto*. Prayer: *Obsecro te*. Virgin and Child enthroned, with four angels, the Virgin's feet on a cushion of gold brocade, and in her hand what appears to be a fruit, an allusion to the sin of Adam redeemed by the blood of Christ. |

Plate X.

Folio 18 recto. Prayer: *Obsecro te*. Virgin and Child enthroned, with four angels, the Virgin's feet on a cushion of gold brocade, and in her hand what appears to be a fruit, an allusion to the sin of Adam redeemed by the blood of Christ.

Plate XI.

Folio 22 verso. Seven Joys of the Virgin Mary. The Assumption of the Virgin, borne by five angels. The nimbed figures are presumably apostles; ten faces are visible, but there appear to be more than twelve haloes.

Plate XII.

Folio 31 verso. Prayer: *O Intemerata*. Pietà scene, with the body of Christ on the knees of the Virgin, St John the Evangelist at his head and Mary Magdalene (recognised by the loose hair and jar of ointment) at his feet; the figure to the Virgin's left is her half-sister Mary Cleophas; Two Holy Women, that on the right without a halo, are also present. *Outer margin*: The Road to Calvary. *Lower margin*: Lamentation of Christ. Joseph of Arimathea and Nicodemus are without haloes. Mary Magdalene is again at Christ's feet, and St John stands next to the Virgin and the Two Holy Women.

Plate XIII.

Folio 36 recto. Matins, Hours of the Virgin. The Annunciation, with four subsidiary scenes. *Bottom left*: The meeting of the Virgin's parents, Joachim and Anne, at the Golden Gate after Joachim's return from exile. *Bottom right*: birth of the Virgin, handed to Anne by a servant. *Right centre*: Presentation of the Virgin at the Temple, greeted by the High Priest. *Top right*: Marriage of Joseph and Mary. The colour of the costumes on the figures here is consistent and helps to identify the people. Joachim is distinguished from Joseph by having a red cloak over a grey undergarment, while Joseph has a grey cloak over a red undergarment; neither is nimbed. However, Anne in the Presentation does not have the white veil as elsewhere. The architectural frames includes figures of Adam and Eve holding fruit.

Plate XIV.

Folio 44 recto. Lauds, Hours of the Virgin. The Visitation. The Virgin, pregnant with Christ, meets St Elizabeth, who reaches out to place her hand on the Virgin's womb. The figure in the background is Elizabeth's husband, Zachariah, struck dumb when he refused to believe the message of the angel Gabriel but recovering his speech when he wrote down his son's name on the latter's birth. *Outer margin*: John the Baptist pointing to his symbol, the Lamb of God. The scene is identical to that on folio 13 recto, and is more relevant to the theme of The Visitation. *Lower margin*: Baptism of Christ by John the Baptist.

Plate XV.

Folio 59 verso. Prime, Hours of the Virgin. Nativity, with two angels and three shepherds. *Bottom right*: Annunciation to the Shepherds, but with no angels shown. *Bottom left*: Moses removing his shoes on learning that he was on holy ground, with a figure of God in the bush, which the illuminator has not shown burning. This scene parallels that of the Nativity in that Moses is being told to lead the Israelites from Egypt to the promised land, just as Christ was to make a path to God. *Left centre*: Three angels with music. *Top left*: figure (king?) with censer before an altar with six candles and a lily, and two other figures. This is possibly a version of the story of Aaron, which included a flowering rod and the levite Korah who was challenged to offer incense to the Lord and was swallowed by the earth for so doing.

Plate XVI.   *Folio 64 recto*. Tierce, Hours of the Virgin. Annunciation to the Shepherds. The dog seems to be a characteristic feature of Rouen Books of Hours of the late fifteenth century. *Outer margin*: Virgin and Child appearing to Caesar Augustus and the Tiburtine Sibyl. According to this legend, known as the *ara coeli*, Roman senators wanted to worship Augustus as God, upon which the prophesy of the Sibyl was sought; this proclaimed that a new king would arrive. The legend is among those brought together by Jacobus of Voraigne in his Golden Legend composed in the thirteenth century. *Bottom margin*: Abraham, about to sacrifice his son Isaac, is prevented by an angel, who points to a ram as a substitute.

Plate XVII.   *Folio 67 recto*. Sext, Hours of the Virgin. Adoration of the Magi. *Outer margin*: a kneeling messenger in front of two standing figures hands a sealed document to a king. This may possibly represent the three Magi before Herod, though they have no marks of royalty. *Bottom margin*: the visit of the Queen of Sheba to Solomon. According to a story popularised by the fourteenth century *Speculum Humanae Salvationis*, Sheba came to Solomon with gifts to ask him questions that would test his wisdom, prefiguring the journey of three Magi.

Plate XVIII.   *Folio 69 verso*. None, Hours of the Virgin. Presentation of Christ in the Temple by the Virgin Mary, Joseph and Two Holy Women. The two doves in the basket refer to the Jewish rite of 'purification' of the mother; they needed to be sacrificed at the same time that shekels were paid to redeem the child presented. *Outer margin*: Presentation of John the Baptist, identified by the lamb held by an attendant. *Lower margin*: Christ Child standing on altar, with High Priest, Virgin Mary and Two Holy Women (perhaps representing Christ disputing in the Temple).

Plate XIX.   *Folio 72 recto*. Vespers, Hours of the Virgin. Flight to Egypt. *Outer margin*: According to legend, the Virgin Mary asked a sower to tell

Herod's soldiers pursuing them that they had passed at sowing time; the corn grew and ripened at once, and the pursuers abandoned the chase on the assumption that the Holy Family had passed some time before. *Lower margin*: Massacre of the Innocents (Herod's soldiers were ordered to kill all children in the hope of disposing of Christ thereby).

Plate XX.

Folio 74 verso. Compline, Hours of the Virgin. Coronation of the Virgin by an angel before God the Father enthroned, with two angels, one of them harping. *Outer margin*: Esther before Xerxes, the Persian king of the fifth century BC. The marriage of the Jewess Esther with Xerxes and her thwarting of a plot to massacre Jews was held to indicate the efficacy of faith in times of need. *Lower margin*: Solomon and Bathsheba, his mother, who was invited by her son to share his throne, an event taken to foreshadow the coronation of the Virgin.

Plate XXI.

Folio 80 recto. Penitential Psalms. David in Penitence, admonished by the prophet Nathan for his adultery with Bathseba and murder of her husband, Uriah the Hittite. Nathan predicted the death of David's child by Bathsheba, and shamed him into removing his crown to pray. *Bottom left*: David slays Goliath. *Bottom centre*: death of Absalom, the son of David who sought to usurp his father's throne; Absalom's hair caught in trees when being pursued by David's troops, and he was lanced as he was suspended. *Bottom right*: David lies on the earth in an effort to save the life of his son by Bathsheba. *Centre right*: Joab, David's general, treacherously slays Abner, a former general of Saul. *Top right*: David watches Bathsheba batheing.

Plate XXII.

Folio 100 recto. Office of the Dead. Encounter of the three living and the three dead. According to an oriental legend first found in France in the thirteenth century, three young men (two of them here shown crowned) returning from a hunt, the most popular pastime of the medieval nobility, met three figures of death who warned them that they too would become like them. *Outer margin*: the Last Judgment, surmounted by God the Father enthroned with saints (Katherine with her wheel and Mary Magdalene with her jar of ointment can be seen among them). *Bottom right*: the Raising of Lazarus. *Bottom left*: Hell-mouth, with two devils stirring a cauldron.

Plate XXIII.

Folio 125 recto. Commendation of Souls. Burial scene, with a shrouded corpse being lowered into the grave by two men, and monks accompanied by mourners in black hoods.

Plate XXIV.

(a) *Folio 138 verso*. Lamentation of Christ. This scene differs from the treatment of the same subject on folio 31 verso (Plate XII). Joseph of Arimathea at Christ's head and Nicodemus at his feet are shown in the same position, but Mary Magdalene, with flowing hair and jar of ointment, stands one figure away from the Virgin Mary.

(b) *Folio 144 verso.* Prayer for the Holy Sacrament of the Altar. God the Father enthroned, holding a chalice with the host. A more suitable illustration at this point might have been of Christ holding chalice and host, especially since an identical picture of God the Father enthroned occurs on folio 149 recto introducing a prayer to Almighty God. The figure here has no stigmata and is bearded.

(c) *Folio 150 recto.* Prayer to the Holy Spirit. Pentecost scene, with the dove descending upon the Apostles and Virgin, who kneel in prayer.

Plate XXV.   *Folio 152 recto.* Psalter of St Jerome. St Jerome in his study, with a lion. St Jerome translated the Bible into Latin in the fourth century, providing the Vulgate version used throughout the middle ages. The story of the lion can be traced back to the thirteenth century Golden Legend. The saint was lecturing on the Bible when a lion limped onto the scene and frightened everyone but Jerome away; the latter removed a thorn from the lion's paw and kept him in his service. The lion was later instrumental in rescuing an ass stolen from the saint.

Plate XXVI.   (a) *Folio 150 verso.* Prayer to the Holy Trinity. The Trinity: God the Father, Christ and the Holy Ghost. Christ is shown bearded but as younger than God the Father, and without the traces of Crucifixion on his hand.

(b) *Folio 167 recto.* Suffrage to St Francis. St Francis receiving the Stigmata. According to the life of St Francis written after his death by St Bonaventura, Francis saw a figure on a crucifix with six wings as he received the marks of Christ's crucifixion, a theme borrowed from the Old Testament Vision of Isaiah. Other parts of the story show Franciscan efforts to stress the conformity between Christ's life and that of Francis.

(c) *Folio 168 recto.* Prayer to Christ's Holy Face. St Veronica with the veil imprinted with Christ's features. The cult of St Veronica and the Holy Face is associated particularly with the fifteenth century and late medieval mysticism.

(d) *Folio 173 verso.* Suffrage to St Christopher. St Christopher wading through the stream carrying the Infant Christ. The hermit who had persuaded Christopher to devote himself to helping the meek and poor is shown with his lantern. The story of St Christopher cannot be traced further back than the eleventh century; the Council of Trent in the sixteenth century tried to suppress his cult, there being no evidence of his historical veracity, but it was not until 1969 that the Catholic Church did this.

Plate XXVII.   *Folio 169 verso.* Plea for Benediction. The Wound in Christ's side (*plaga lateris Christi*), in chalice held by two angels, against the three nails of the Crucifixion. In a small number of late fifteenth century Books of Hours, the Wound is illustrated 'according to what was revealed to Denis of *Bargona*'. Pictures of the Wound of Christ in a chalice were included in late fifteenth century printed Books of Hours (J. Harthan, *Books of Hours*, 1977, p.170; W.P. Simpson, 'On the measure of the Wound in the Side of the Redeemer', *Journal of the British Archaeological Association*, vol.XXX, 1874, pp.357–374).

Plate XXVIII.   *Folio 170 verso.* Prayer to Christ. The Instruments of the Passion. The late middle ages saw the multiplication of these instruments; here we see the coins given to Judas at the foot of the column to which Christ was tied with the rope and flagellated with the whip; the cock refers to St Peter's denial; on the right are the hammer for attaching the nails and the pincers to remove them, the ewer and basin in which Pontius Pilate washed his hands, the hand that struck Christ, the sponge on a stick and a bucket for the vinegar, the sword by which St Peter struck off the ear of Malchus when Judas betrayed Christ, Christ's garment and the dice which were thrown to see to whom it should be given.

Plate XXIX.   *Folio 174 verso.* Suffrage to St George. St George killing the dragon. The cult of St George grew with the development of chivalry and the romance literature associated with it. From the early thirteenth century, he was the national saint of England (the Synod of Oxford of 1222 was an important landmark), but his cult was also widespread in continental Europe.

Plate XXX.   *Folio 176 recto.* Suffrage of St Thomas a Becket of Canterbury. Martyrdom of St Thomas of Canterbury. Thomas a Becket was canonised only three years after his death in 1170. His cult was widespread in England and in northern France. He was declared a traitor and a rebel by Henry VIII, who ordered the destruction of images of the saint and the supression of his cult in 1538. Many Books of Hours that survive in England have all reference to this saint excised.

Plate XXXI.   *Folio 182 recto.* Suffrage to St Apollonia. Apollonia of Alexandria was said to have had her teeth brutally extracted before being thrown onto a fire in 249 AD.

Plate XXXII.   *Folio 202 recto.* St John's Account of the Passion. Crucifixion, with Mary Magdalene wiping the feet of Christ (prefigured by her annointment of Christ's feet in the house of Simon the Pharisee), and blood issuing from the Wound in Christ's side towards the Virgin Mary. On the right, Joseph of Arimathea remonstrates with a soldier.

14. *List of Figures*

119

15. *Footnotes*

1. For a survey, see J. Harthan, *Books of Hours and their owners* (1977), which discusses 34 such manuscripts; an essential account of books of this kind can be found in the introduction to V. Leroquais, *Les Livres d'Heures manuscrits de la Bibliothèque Nationale*, 3 vols. (1927) and supplement (1943). Statistics of printed Books of Hours can be found in H. Bohatta, *Bibliographie der Livres d'Heures des XV und XVI Jahrhunderts* (Vienna, 1924); see also A. Labarre, *Le livre dans la vie amiénoise du 16ᵉ siècle* (1971), p.41.

2. J. Blackhouse, 'French manuscript illumination, 1450–1530', in *Renaissance Painting in Manuscripts. Treasures from the British Library*, ed. T. Kren (1983), p.145.

3. L.M.J. Delaissé, The importance of Books of Hours for the history of the medieval book', *Gatherings in Honor of Dorothy E. Miner*, ed. U.E. McCracken *et al.* (Baltimore, [1974]), pp.203–225.

4. P. Benedict, *Rouen during the Wars of Religion* (Cambridge, 1981), p.3; *Histoire de Rouen*, ed. M. Mollat (1979), p.159; P. Chanu and R. Gascon, *Histoire Economique et Sociale de la France. I: de 1450 à 1660* (1977), pp.408–9; R. Gandilhon, *Politique économique de Louis XI* (1941), pp.203, 223, 282–3.

5. J. Dewald, *The formation of a provincial nobility. The magistrates of the Parlement of Rouen, 1499–1610* (Princeton, 1980).

6. Names of these officials from 1463 onwards were published by L. Delisle, *Catalogue des livres imprimés ou publiés à Caen. Tome second: Recherches sur les imprimeurs et les libraires*, vol.XXIV (1904) of the *Bulletin de la Société des Antiquaires de Normandie*, pp.cxxi–cxxix.

7. The cathedral archives are calendared in detail in the *Inventaire Sommaire des Archives Départementales antérieures à 1790. Seine Inférieure. Archives Ecclésiastiques*, série G, tome II (1874), hereafter cited as *Inv.Som.Arch.Dép.*, série G, II.

8. For Georges d'Amboise, archbishop 1499–1510, and his nephew of the same name, archbishop 1511–1550, both of them significant for patronage of Renaissance artists, see Jouen, *Comptes, devis et inventaires du manoir archiépiscopal de Rouen* (1908), pp.385–392 and 423–428; for payments to scribes and illuminators made in 1502 by Georges d'Amboise (d.1510), see A. Deville, *Comptes et dépenses de la construction du Château de Gaillon* (1850), pp.437–444. A. Blunt, *Art and architecture in France, 1500–1700* (1953), discusses the works of both archbishops.

9. Paris. Bibliothèque Nationale, ms. latin 1169; see Leroquais, *Livres d'Heures*, vol. I, p.96.

10. J.J.G. Alexander, 'A lost leaf from a Bodleian Book of Hours', *Bodleian Library Record*, vol.VIII, no.5 (1971), pp.248–251; J. Plummer, *The last flowering. French painting in manuscripts, 1420–1530* (1982), pp.90–96; G. Ritter and J. Lafond, *Manuscrits à peintures de l'école de Rouen. Livres d'Heures normands* (1913). The most extensive discussion of problems connected with the Rouen 'school' is that of E. König, *Stundenbuch des markgrafen Christoph I von Baden. Codex Durlach I der Badischen Landesbibliothek* (Karlsruhe, 1978), pp.163 et *seq.*

11. C. de Beaurepaire, *Derniers mélanges historiques ... concernant le département de la Seine-Inférieure* (Rouen, 1909), pp.229–235. These extracts from muniments in the *Archives Départementales* at Rouen can be supplemented by the *Inventaire Sommaire* mentioned in note 7 above. See also the work by Jouen mentioned in note 8 above. For sixteenth century goldsmiths in Rouen by the name of Du Moustier, see C.–G. Cassan, *Les orfèvres de la Normandie du XVI au XIX siècles* (1980), p.213.

12. C. de Beaurepaire, *Derniers mélanges*, p.230; *Inv.Som.Arch.Dép.*, série G, II, pp.243, 253–6. Scribes can probably be taken to have written by hand the kind of ephemeral notices later supplied by printers: the latter are described in G. Lepreux, *Gallia Typographica ... Série Départementale, tome III: Province de Normandie*, part 1 (1912), p.87 n.8.

13. C. de Beaurepaire, *Nouveaux mélanges historiques et archéologiques* (Rouen, 1904), pp.209–211; C. de Beaurepaire, *Derniers mélanges*, p.231; For the topography and street names of Rouen, see P. Periaux, *Dictionnaire indicateur des rues et places de Rouen* (Rouen, 1819).

14. R. Gandhilon, *Politique économique de Louis XI* (1941), pp.96, 168.

15. P. Delalain, *Étude sur le libraire parisien du XIII au XV siècle* (1891); *Ordonnances des Rois de France*, 23 vols. (1723–1849), vol.XVI, pp.669–71; P. Chauvet, *Les ouvriers du livre en France, des origines à 1789* (1959), pp.7–10.

16. C. Ouin-La Croix, *Histoire des anciens corporations d'arts et métiers et des confréries religieuses de la Normandie* (Rouen, 1850), p.145; P. Chevreux & J. Vernier, *Les archives de Normandie et de la Seine Inférieure. État général des fonds* (1911), p.8; P. Benedict, *Rouen during the Wars of Religion* (Cambridge, 1981), pp.6–7; *L'Entrée de Henri II à Rouen, 1550*, Facsimile with introduction by M.M. McGowan (New York: Johnson Reprint Corporation, [c.1974]). Earlier accounts of *entrées* into Rouen, the first dated 1485, are published by the *Société des Bibliophiles Normands* and do not contain any 'occupational census' of the city's inhabitants. There is a possibility that a confraternity bringing together illuminators and book producers existed in fifteenth century Rouen; large numbers of confraternities are recorded as having financed prayers and masses in the cathedral and elsewhere, but the link between their members appears not to be mentioned (L. Martin, *Répertoire des anciennes confréries et charités du diocèse de Rouen ... de 1435 à 1610*, Fécamp, 1936).

17. C. de Beaurepaire, *Nouveaux mélanges* (Rouen, 1904), pp.360–366; *Inv.Som.Arch. Dép., série G, II*, pp.215, 244.

18. This contract was published by C. de Beaurepaire, *Nouveaux mélanges* (Rouen, 1904), p.360, from the archives of the 'tabellionage de Rouen, Régistre 18, folio 215 verso'.

19. C. de Beaurepaire, *Derniers mélanges* (Rouen, 1909), p.230.

20. This paragraph relies on information in the calendars to be found in *Inv.Som., Arch.Dép., série G, II*, pp.215 et seq., and 351 et seq. The presence of booksellers is worth recording, since many large cities in France appear to have had none while at the same time counting book producers among their inhabitants; see L. Royer, 'Bibliothèques, écrivains en lettre de forme, enlumineurs et relieurs à Grenoble aux XIVᵉ et XVᵉ siècles', *Petite Revue des Bibliophiles Dauphinois*, 2ᵉ série, tome IV, no.2 (1935), p.13.

21. In 1540, Claude Leroy was '*libraire tenant la première eshoppe aux degrés du Palais de Rouen*', while in 1551 Martin Le Megissier had his shop ('*boutique*') '*aux degrés du Palais de Rouen*' (G. Lepreux, *Gallia Typograhica . . . Série Départementale, tome III: Province de Normandie*, part 1 (1912), pp.256, 259.

22. C. de Beaurepaire, *Nouveaux mélanges* (Rouen, 1904), pp.362–6; *Derniers mélanges* (Rouen, 1909), pp.231, 235; *Inv.Som.Arch.Dép., Série G, II*, pp.215, 356.

23. P. Renouard, *Documents sur les imprimeurs, libraires . . . enlumineurs . . . ayant exercé à Paris de 1450 à 1600* (1901), p.24.

24. C. de Beaurepaire, *Nouveaux mélanges* (Rouen, 1904), p.360; P. Pansier, *Histoire du livre . . . à Avignon du XIV au XVI siècle* (1922), vol.III, pp.65–6.

25. For this paragraph, see the references in note 20 above and C. Couderc, 'Fragments relatifs à André Le Musnier, libraire-juré de l'Université de Paris', *Bulletin de la Société de l'Histoire de Paris et de l'Ile de France*, vol.XLV (1918), pp.90–107; the documents published in this article were used as scrap paper to strengthen a binding. I am grateful to Michael Gullick for pointing this article out to me.

26. See note 20 above and also E. Frere, *De l'imprimerie à Rouen dans les XV et XVI siècles* (Rouen, 1843), pp.5–7.

27. P. Le Verdier, *L'Atelier de Guillaume Le Talleur* (1916). People described as citizens of Rouen worked as printers in Italy, Switzerland and eastern France from the 1470s.

28. *Inv.Som.Arch.Dép., Série G, II*, pp.356, 358 (Gaillat's second shop was specifically said to sell printed books, '*livres en molle*'); *Catalogue of books printed in the XVth century now in the British Museum* (1949), pp.392–3; Delisle, *Catalogue des livres imprimés . . . à Caen*, vol.XXIII (1903), pp.328–9.

29. Delisle, *op.cit.*, vol.XXIII (1903), pp.82, 158, 225, 264, 266, 280; 179.

30. U. Baurmeister, 'Was Jacques Le Forestier the printer of the *Horae ad usum Sarum* of 1495?', *British Library Journal*, vol.9, no.1 (1983), pp.66–75; E. Armstrong, 'English purchases of printed books from the Continent, 1465–1526', *English Historical Review*, vol.94 (1979), p.278.

31. See E. Frere, *Des livres de liturgie des églises d'Angleterre (Salisbury, York, Hereford)*, *imprimés à Rouen dans les XV et XVI siècles* (Rouen, 1867). For the careers of Pynson and de Machlinia, see the *Dictionary of National Biography*.

32. I owe my knowledge of the Cambridge manuscript, and of that in The Hague, entirely to the kindness of Mr John Higgitt.

33. Paris, Bibliothèque Nationale, ms. latin 18030. M François Avril was kind enough to bring this manuscript to my attention. Delaissé remarked that a number of Books of Hours of Coutances Use bear all the marks of having been made in Rouen ('The importance of Books of Hours', *Gatherings in Honour of Dorothy E. Miner* [1974], p.221), demonstrating the city's predominance in the book trade within Normandy.

34. *Catalogue of books printed in the XVth century now in the British Museum* (1949), p.395.

35. The binding is that on Paris, Bibliothèque Nationale, ms. latin 1107, a late thirteenth century Missal of St Denis rebound for the abbey in the fifteenth; a facsimile of the piece of parchment is published in C. Samaran, 'Manuscrits "imposés" à la manière typographique', *Mélanges en Hommage à la Mémoire de Fr. Martroye* (1940), pp.325–336, plate XIX. I am grateful to Mr Nicholas Rogers for identifying the Use for me. This technique of producing handwritten books is discussed by L. Gilissen, *Prolégomènes à la codicologie* (1977).

36. See the article by Couderc mentioned in note 25 (pp.97–98); E. König, 'The influence of the invention of printing on the development of German illumination', *Manuscripts in the Fifty Years after the Invention of Printing*, ed. J.B. Trapp (1983), p.85; E. König, 'A leaf from a Gutenberg Bible illuminated in England', *British Library Journal*, vol.9, no.1 (Spring 1983), pp.32–50.

37. The manuscript did not appear in the catalogue of the sale held by the British Red Cross Society on 8 April 1918 and following days; it was offered for sale by Dr Playfair in June of that year, and the profits went to the St Andrew's section of the British Red Cross (Scottish Branch); see *The Times*, 18 July 1918.

38. I am most grateful to Mirjam Foot for information on this point, and for her comments on the binding.

39. For other bindings with similar strapwork with an admixture of arabesque ornament and areas of dotted gold, see G.D. Hobson, *Bindings in Cambridge Libraries* (1929), plate XXX (Paris, *c.*1560); H.M. Nixon, *Sixteenth-century gold-tooled book-*

bindings in the *Pierpont Morgan Library* (1971), nos.25 and 26 (both Paris, *c*.1552); O. Pächt & D. Thoss, *Die illuminierten Handschriften und Inkunabeln der österreichischen Nationalbibliothek: französische Schule*, II, part 2 (plates), Abb.302 (Book of Hours, Lyons, late fifteenth century: Cod.s.n.2598).

40. The arms are (i) Barry of 6, argent and sable [the sable appears to have been painted over gules], (ii) Argent, 3 bars gules.

41. This manuscript is described in M.R. James, *Bibliotheca Pepysiana. A descriptive catalogue of the library of Samuel Pepys [Magdalene College, Cambridge]. Part III: Medieval Manuscripts* (London, 1923), pp.14–19. Details of Lord Hay of Yester can be found in *Calendar of writs preserved at Yester House, 1166–1625*, compiled by C.C. Harvey & J. MacLeod, vol.55 of the *Scottish Record Society* (1935), p.85.

42. For a brief description and reproduction of the scene of the Annunciation to the Shepherds, see *Liturgische handschriften uit de Koninklijke Bibliotheek* (The Hague: Rijksmuseum Meermanno-Westreenianum, 1983), pp.36, 67. For Sanquhar and Farmor, see G.E.C., *The Complete Peerage*, vol.III (1913), p.541, and the *Dictionary of National Biography* under 'Crichton'.

43. See R. Watson, 'Medieval manuscript fragments', *Archives*, vol.XIII, no.58 (1977), p.71; A.N.L. Munby, *Connoisseurs and medieval miniatures, 1750–1850* (Oxford, 1972), pp.158–160, and *passim*.

44. For texts used in Books of Hours, see the introduction to volume I of V. Leroquais, *Les Livres d'Heures manuscrits de la Bibliothèque Nationale* (1927).

45. V. Leroquais, *Les Livres d'Heures manuscrits de la Bibliothèque Nationale*, vol.I (1927), p.87; A. Collette, *Histoire du Bréviaire de Rouen* (Rouen, 1902), p.177; R.W. Pfaff, *New liturgical feasts in later medieval England* (Oxford, 1970), pp.29–30, 34.

46. Pfaff, *New liturgical feasts* (1970), pp.46, 76–77, 93 *et seq*.

47. The name Dufour appears in fifteenth century Rouen (Jouen, *Comptes, devis et inventaires du manoir archiépiscopal de Rouen*, 1908, p.282); a Jean Dufour had a career as *Greffier* of the *Cour des Aides de Normandie* between 1523 and 1546 when he died, and may have been the 'Jean Dufour l'ainé' mentioned in 1532 as a bourgeois of Rouen (*Catalogue des actes de François I*, vols.IV, no.11024, V, no.15160, VI, nos.20397, 23154, 22976, VII, nos.23796–7). The most likely candidate is Jean Dufour, fourth son of Jean Dufour *l'ainé*, *échevin* of Rouen in 1522, who married 'N . . . Dantan' and whose eldest son was himself married in 1609. 'Dantan' could easily be a false transcription of 'd'Autin', and an 'M' misread as an 'N'. (H. de Frondeville, *Les conseillers du parlement de Normandie au seizième siècle*, Paris & Rouen: Société de l'Histoire de Normandie, 1960, p.335). A goldsmith by the name of Claude Austin was in Rouen in 1604 (M.P.Le Cacheux, *Répertoire numérique des Archives du Département de la Seine Inférieure . . . Série H, Tome IV: St Ouen de Rouen (14H1–14H926)*,

Rouen, 1938, p.124). Each page of Antiquaries 13 has a letter in sequence to make up the names of Jean Dufour and Marguerite Austin when turned over consecutively; however, these letters appear to be painted over older letters which can occasionally be made out, giving the name 'ELISABE[TH]......O.ASI.IO..'. So the Jean and Marguerite whose names are visible may have had their names entered on a manuscript inherited in the latter half of the sixteenth century.

48. N.R. Ker, *Medieval Manuscripts in British Libraries*, vol.II (Oxford, 1977), pp.595–6; O. Pächt & D. Thoss, *Die illuminierten Handschriften und Inkunabeln der österreichischen Nationalbibliothek: französische Schule I* (Vienna, 1974), plates 293–301.

49. W. Werner, *Cimelia Heidelbergensia. 30 illuminierte Handschriften der Universitätsbibliothek Heidelberg* (Wiesbaden, 1975), pp.19–23 (no.3), with plate of January illustration; M. Meiss, *French painting in the time of Jean de Berry: the Boucicaut Master* (1968), plates 242 & 243.

50. E.P. Spencer, *The Sobieski Hours. A manuscript in the Royal Library at Windsor Castle* (London [Roxburghe Club], 1977), plates i to xxiv.

51. M. Meiss, *French painting in the time of Jean de Berry. The Limbourgs and their contemporaries* (1974), plate 562.

52. L.M.J. Delaissé, J. Marrow & J. de Wit, *The James A. de Rothschild Collection at Waddesdon Manor. Illuminated Manuscripts* (1977), p.130.

53. J. Lafond, *Un Livre d'Heures rouennais enluminé d'après le* Speculum Humanae Salvationis (Rouen, 1929), plate X.

54. J. Plummer, *The last flowering. French painting in manuscripts, 1420–1530* (1982) [catalogue of an exhibition at the Pierpont Morgan Library, New York], p.17 (no.24). I am grateful to John Plummer for sending me copies of miniatures in Pierpont Morgan Library, M.220.

55. The Nativity in two Rouen Use Books of Hours in North America, Cleveland Museum of Art, MS.52.227, and Princeton University, Art Museum, MS.51–35, is again closely related to these scenes, though the marginal decoration of each is quite different; see A. Stones & J. Steyaert, *Medieval illumination, glass and sculpture in Minnesota collections* (Minneapolis: University of Minnesota, 1978), p.83; *Bulletin of the Cleveland Museum of Art*, no.44 (1957), frontispiece of Nativity scene in colour. I am grateful to Mr John Higgit for this reference.

56. D. François Hue, *La communauté des chirurgiens de Rouen ... 1407–1791* (Rouen, 1913), colour plates between pp.44 & 45 and 62 & 63. The figures are painted in a Renaissance style, with graceful poses and modelled in the round; the walls that serve as backgrounds, and the architectural canopies show the survival of conventions used before 1500.

57. Delaissé *et al*, *The James A. de Rothschild Collection . . . Illuminated Manuscripts* (1977), p.551; other manuscripts related to Waddesdon 25 are mentioned on p.560.

58. For the manuscript from which the name is derived, see *L'Enluminure de Charlemagne à François Ier* (Geneva, 1976) [catalogue of an exhibition held in the Musée Rath, Geneva], pp.115–117 (no.49). The manuscript is said to be of the third quarter of the fifteenth century, and made at Rouen.

59. *The last flowering* (1982), p.67 (no.88) and plate.

60. Ritter & Lafond, *Manuscrits à peintures de l'école de Rouen* (1913), plate LXVI.

61. The following pictures are reproduced in the catalogue: the Betrayal, Decapitation of John the Baptist, John the Evangelist on Patmos, Martyrdom of St Thomas a Becket, St Martin of Tours. I am told by Claudia Rabel that this is the manuscript described by A. Bachelin, *Description du Livre d'Heures du prieuré de Saint-Lô de Rouen* (Paris, 1869), with plates of folios 134 verso (owner praying before an angel) and 85 verso (funeral service).

62. Apart from references in notes 10 & 50, see also L. Williams, 'A Rouen Book of Hours of the Sarum Use, *c*.1444, belonging to Thomas Lord Hoo', *Proceedings of the Royal Irish Academy*, vol.75, section C (1975), pp.189–212, plates VI–XXI.

63. J. Porcher, *French miniatures from illuminated manuscripts* (1960), p.75.

64. *The last flowering* (1982), p.66.